The Lab

C000284848

Contents

www.labour.org.uk

Britain *forward* not back

Preface Tony Blair

New Labour's 2005 manifesto applies the unchanging values of our party to the new priorities of the British people. It is a plan to improve the lives of hard-working families and prepare our country for success in a fast-changing world. Our case rests on one idea more than any other – that it is the duty of government to provide opportunity and security for all in a changing world. Every chapter relates back to that goal: breaking down the barriers that stop people fulfilling their talent, extending opportunity to every corner of the United Kingdom, building communities strong and safe for those who play by the rules. On the firm foundations we have laid since 1997, our programme will embed a new progressive consensus in our country.

This preface is my personal message.

Eight years ago, I offered new leadership – fresh, idealistic, energetic, but untested. You voted for change and gave me the chance to serve. In our first term we banished the demons of ten per cent interest rates, mass unemployment, wages of £1.50 an hour, and outside toilets in our schools. We put Labour values into action. And we banished Labour demons too: we showed we could run the economy well, cut crime, and stand up for Britain abroad. We proved our competence.

Four years ago, I said we needed to continue the modernisation of our economy, coupled with investment and reform to achieve change in public services. At the end of this second term we have delivered an unprecedented period of stability and growth, we have increased investment and we have embarked on a radical programme of reform to put the people themselves in the driving seat of our public services. We have made difficult decisions – about health policy, student finance, and secondary school reform. In the process we have proved our resilience. Now we go to the people not only having delivered on our promises, but also setting new and more ambitious goals for our public services and our country.

But Britain can be better still.

I know the change is possible. Not just because I have studied the statistics, but because I have seen it with my own eyes, across the length and breadth of the United Kingdom.

I have spoken to NHS staff in Coventry, Edinburgh and Swansea, who tell me how their new hospital and the new funding is letting them improve care for their patients.

I have heard teachers in Bexley, Middlesbrough and Sheffield tell me how they no longer have to work in crumbling classrooms without books and computers – and pupils show me, with pride, round their sparkling new school.

I have met youngsters in Blackpool and London whose lives have been transformed by the New Deal – once written off, they are now full of confidence and ambition.

I've been to communities in Southampton and Darlington where the Sure Start programme is helping overcome disadvantage and seen for myself the remarkable revival of our great cities.

I have met aid workers in Africa who tell me how this country is improving the lives of the poorest on our planet.

These are not the fantasy of politicians. They are the stories of real life in our country and abroad. Not for everyone. Not everywhere. But for enough people and in enough places for us to know it is not a fluke. Personal prosperity and the good society; the fruit of partnership between the British people and a government on their side.

Now we have to decide whether to go forward or back.

Britain is on the right track. We will not change direction. Neither will we rest on our laurels. Our third-term opportunity is to build on the progress we have made. That progress, first as a party then in government began with the insight that the only way to advance decent progressive values was to develop a new policy agenda. Our understanding of the world and the great changes underway in our society led us to reject the false choices of the past. This is the foundation stone of new Labour.

I believe that in our third term we can embed a new progressive consensus. One that reflects the mission of our movement, and the hopes and values of our people. And as much as the pursuit of this consensus represents an unprecedented opportunity for progressive politics, so it will be bitterly opposed by those who seek to take us back to the divisions of the past.

In our third term we will forge an even stronger bond between the goals of economic progress and social justice. No going back to fiscal irresponsibility. No going back to a Conservative government that says mass unemployment is a price worth paying. Going forward instead to an opportunity economy, spreading prosperity through high employment and welfare reform, spreading opportunity through widening access to university and training, spreading ownership through the Child Trust Fund and expanding homeownership.

In our third term we will make public services safe for a generation. No going back to one-size-fits-all monolithic services. No going back to the Tory years of cuts and privatisation. Going forward instead to services free to all, personal to each: breaking once and for all the drop-out culture in education and the waiting-list culture in health, by raising investment and driving innovation through diversity of provision and power in the hands of the patient, the parent and the citizen.

In our third term we will cement a new social contract with rights matched by responsibilities. No going back to 'no such thing as society'. Going forward instead to power and resources in the hands of the law-abiding majority. A government committed both to abolishing child poverty and to putting the values of individual responsibility and duty at the very heart of policy.

In our third term we will show that our national interest can only be pursued by engaging with the world's great challenges. No going back to a Britain marginalised and weak. Going forward to a stronger country in a safer, fairer world. Leading on Africa, leading on the environment, at the heart of Europe, working together to tackle terror and spread peace and justice.

We do not duck the tough choices – from independence for the Bank of England to the tax rise we made for the NHS, to the war in Iraq. We made decisions because we believed them right – not because they were destined to be popular.

But we refuse to accept false choices. The British people never wanted to choose between wealth creation and social justice. They never wanted to choose between national security and overseas aid. They never wanted to choose between equal rights and protection from crime. These are the false choices that landed us with economic decline and social division.

The British people have the capacity to make this a great country. Our ideals are undimmed: extend opportunity to all, demand responsibility from all, secure justice for all. Our policies are refreshed: never has a governing party proposed a more wide-ranging programme of change for the country. Our vision is clear: a country more equal in its opportunities, more secure in its communities, more confident in its future. It is our social contract: we help you, you help yourself; you benefit and the country benefits.

So now, I fight my last election as Leader of my party and Prime Minister of our country. My call is a passionate one: let's together make irreversible the positive changes that are happening in our country. Let's make the values of social justice and a fair deal for all the governing ideal of our country not just for some time but for all time. People freed from barriers of class, building a better future for themselves and for the country. Self-interest and national interest together.

Britain
forward
not back

New Labour's record:
The contract delivered
Our country is changing for
the better, because we fulfilled
the promises of our 1997 and
2001 manifestos. Here is what
has changed.

■ Prosperity for all

Britain now has a stable, growing economy with the lowest inflation since the 1960s.

Since 1997, two million more people are in work, and the UK has the lowest unemployment for 30 years. Tax credits and the minimum wage are ensuring that work pays for everyone.

Because of this we are saving £5 billion a year on the costs of unemployment – that's £84 for every citizen in Britain – money that is being invested in frontline services such as schools and hospitals.

There are over one million more homeowners, saving on average nearly £4,000 a year, thanks to the lowest mortgage rates for 40 years.

Since 1997, average incomes have increased by 19 per cent and the income of a typical family has increased by 17 per cent, with living standards rising in double digits for every part of the income spectrum.

There are 300,000 more businesses, providing jobs and increased prosperity.

There are two million fewer children and nearly two million fewer pensioners living in absolute poverty.

■ World-class public services

Investment in public services is up – an extra £1,000 per pupil per year in real terms since 1997, and spending on the NHS has more than doubled to £69 billion. There are over 28,000 more teachers and 105,000 extra teaching assistants and support staff. The National Health Service now has 79,000 more nurses and over 27,000 more doctors. And public servants – from nurses to police officers – are better rewarded for their work.

Our ten-year-old pupils are ranked third best in the world in literacy and are the fastest improving in numeracy.

Since the introduction of free entry, visits to our national museums and galleries have risen by 75 per cent.

Deaths from heart disease are down by 27 per cent and cancer deaths are down by 12 per cent.

■ A modern welfare state

Thanks to our New Deal, long-term youth unemployment has been virtually eradicated, with over half a million young people helped into work.

By October 2005, families with children will be on average £1,400 a year better off as a result of our tax and benefit measures compared to 1997.

Thanks to our reforms pensioner households are on average £1,500 a year better off, rising to £2,000 for the poorest third.

Maternity leave has increased to 26 weeks and maternity pay has almost doubled.

There are 1.2 million more older people in employment. The employment rate for people aged between 50 and pension age has increased by over five percentage points to 70 per cent.

■ Strong and safe communities

Crime has fallen by 30 per cent overall, with almost five million fewer crimes a year than in 1997.

There are record numbers of police, nearly 13,000 more, assisted by 4,600 new Community Support Officers.

New powers to tackle anti-social behaviour have been introduced, with nearly 4,000 Anti-Social Behaviour Orders issued so far and nearly 66,000 fixed penalty notices.

We have halved the time from arrest to sentencing for persistent young offenders.

More than 80 per cent of initial decisions on asylum claims are now processed in two months.

■ Britain strong in the world

Britain's interests are at the heart of an enlarged European Union, with economic reform putting jobs first.

Our international aid budget for the world's poorest countries has more than doubled.

We have successfully pressed for the restarting of world trade talks which will focus on the needs of developing countries.

Our strong, effective and responsive armed forces are ensuring the defence of Britain's interests.

We introduced greenhouse-gas trading to cut pollution – the first country to do so – reducing emissions by 9.8 million tonnes in the first two years.

Chapter 1
Economy: Rising prosperity in an opportunity society
Forward to increased prosperity, not back to boom and bust

1979-1997: Interest rates average over ten per cent

1997-2005: Britain, the fourth largest economy in the world, with the longest ever period of continuous growth

2010: Full employment in every region and nation

Labour's economic record is unprecedented – the highest employment ever, longest period of uninterrupted growth in modern history, lowest sustained interest and inflation rates for a generation. Our economic policies will build on the platform of stability and growth in three ways: entrenching a low-debt/high-employment economy which generates investment in public services; supporting enterprise and wealth creation by making Britain the best place to do business; and helping every part of Britain and every person in Britain to contribute to and gain from the strength of our economy. And as we work globally to tackle climate change we recognise the challenge and the opportunity of achieving sustainable development at home.

■ The new Labour case

Our economic record has finally laid to rest the view that Labour could not be trusted with the economy. We are winning the argument that economic dynamism and social justice must go hand in hand. In the future the countries that do best will be those with a shared purpose about the long-term changes and investments they need to make – and have the determination to equip their people for that future. So, we approach new challenges with a progressive strategy for growth. In our third term we will build new ladders of social mobility and advancement on the firm foundations of stability, investment and growth.

■ Low debt and high employment

In the last eight years we have pioneered a British way to economic stability. Our economy has grown in every quarter with this Government. Interest rates have averaged 5.3 per cent since 1997, saving mortgage payers on average nearly £4,000 per year compared to the Tory years.

Only with Labour, which constructed this framework, will this continue. We will maintain our inflation target at two per cent. We will

15

continue to meet our fiscal rules: over the economic cycle, we will borrow only to invest, and keep net debt at a stable and prudent level.

▮ Public spending and taxation

The longest period of uninterrupted economic growth in modern times has enabled the Government to deliver the longest period of sustained investment in public services for a generation. Social security bills for unemployment have been halved since 1997, saving £5 billion a year, and we are also saving £4 billion a year on debt interest payments. Over the ten-year period 1997-98 to 2007-08, real-terms investment per year in education will have risen by 4.8 per cent and in health by 6.5 per cent.

> *'We are winning the argument that economic dynamism and social justice must go hand in hand.'*

Every pound we invest goes further because of our drive for efficiency and reform. Labour will complete the implementation of Sir Peter Gershon's recommendations to improve public-service efficiency and root out waste, liberating over £21 billion for investment in front-line services.

Labour believes tax policy should continue to be governed by the health of the public finances, the requirement for public investment and the needs of families, business and the environment.

We will not raise the basic or top rates of income tax in the next Parliament. We renew our pledge not to extend VAT to food, children's

clothes, books, newspapers and public transport fares. We will continue to make targeted tax cuts for families and to support work. As a
result of personal tax and benefit measures introduced since 1997, by
October 2005 families with children will be on average £1,400 a year
better off in real terms. Living standards in Britain have been rising, on
average, by 2.5 per cent per year since 1997 – a total increase of
nearly 20 per cent.

We want a tax regime that supports British business. That is why we
have cut corporation tax to its lowest ever level, introduced the best
regime of capital gains tax in any industrialised country, and introduced a new Research and Development tax credit.

■ Full employment

Our goal is employment opportunity for all – the modern definition of
full employment. Britain has more people in work than ever before,
with the highest employment rate in the G7. Our long-term aim is to
raise the employment rate to 80 per cent. And, as we move more people from welfare to work, the savings on unemployment benefits will
go towards investing more in education.

We will make work pay. With Labour's tax credits a family with two
children pays no net tax until their earnings reach £21,000.

We will implement the recommendations of the Low Pay Commission
to raise the minimum wage to £5.05 from October 2005 and £5.35
from October 2006.

The New Deals and the creation of JobCentre Plus have made a major
contribution to cutting unemployment. The active welfare state
created since 1997 is working.

The Tories trebled the number on incapacity benefits. We will help people who can work into rehabilitation and eventually into employment, recognising the practical assistance to disabled people of the Access to Work scheme. We will build on the successful Pathways to Work programme and reform Incapacity Benefit, with the main elements of the new benefit regime in place from 2008. The majority of claimants with more manageable conditions will be required to engage in both work-focused interviews and in activity to help them prepare for a return to work. Those with the most severe conditions will also be encouraged to engage in activity and should receive more money than now. We will continue to welcome new independent and voluntary sector partners to provide job-seeking services.

■ Supporting enterprise

Government does not create wealth but it must support the wealth creators. That is why our priorities are the national infrastructure of skills, science, regulation and planning, and transport. The economy of the future will be based on knowledge, innovation and creativity. That applies both to manufacturing and services.

In a fast changing global economy, government cannot postpone or prevent change. The modern role for government – the case for a modern employment and skills policy – is to equip people to succeed, to be on their side, helping them become more skilled, adaptable and flexible for the job ahead rather than the old Tory way of walking away leaving people unaided to face change.

Successful manufacturing industries are vital to our future prosperity. The Labour Government backs manufacturing: from launch investment for Airbus A380 Super Jumbo to the successful Manufacturing Advisory Service helping 13,000 of our smaller manufacturing businesses in its first year. In a third term we will continue to do so.

Public procurement is a big opportunity for business in Britain and

'In our third term we will build new ladders of social mobility and advancement on the firm foundations of stability, investment and growth.'

the source of many jobs. We will promote a public procurement strategy that safeguards UK jobs and skills, under EU rules, to ensure that British industry can compete fairly with the rest of Europe.

Britain has some of the strongest capital markets in the world. We are determined they – and our financial services industry – should prosper. We will ensure that companies have the right framework of corporate governance and relationships with the institutions that invest our pension funds and savings in them.

■ Skills at work

Our reforms to 14-19 education (see chapter 2) will raise the quality and quantity of apprenticeships and vocational education. We are now putting in place a comprehensive and ambitious strategy to help everyone get on at work:

* *All adults to get free access to basic skills in literacy, language and numeracy.*
* *A new national programme, working with employers, to ensure that employees who did not reach GCSE standard (level 2) at school will get time off for free training up to level 2.*
* *A new partnership between government and employers to fund workplace training at level 3 (technician level)*
* *A genuinely employer-driven training system – in every sector there will be a Sector Skills Council determining the training strategy and a leading edge Skills Academy.*
* *A nationwide system of advice – bringing together support on skills, jobs and careers – helping people to get on at work.*
* *A strong partnership with trade unions to boost workplace training including a new TUC Academy and continued support for Union Learning Reps.*

■ Supporting science

The alliance of scientific research and business creativity is key to our continued prosperity.

Looking ahead, we are committed to a ten-year strategy on science and innovation that will continue to invest in our science and industrial base at least in line with trend GDP. Our ambition now is to raise the UK's total private and public sector investment in research and development, as a proportion of national income, from its current 1.9 per cent to 2.5 per cent by 2014.

Our pharmaceutical and biotechnology industries are world leaders. We have created one of the world's best environments for stem-cell research. We have now passed legislation to protect our researchers from the activities of animal rights extremists.

Across a range of environmental issues – from soil erosion to the depletion of marine resources, from water scarcity to air pollution – it is clear now not just that economic activity is their cause but that these problems in themselves threaten future economic activity and growth. We will continue to work with the environmental goods and services sector – which is already worth £25 billion to the economy to promote new green technologies and industries in the UK and internationally, and use the purchasing power of government to support environmental improvement.

■ Competition, planning and regulation

Competition is à driving force for innovation. Our competition regime has been toughened with independent competition bodies and stronger penalties.

To the benefit of business and household consumers we are liberalising the postal services market, while protecting the universal service at a uniform tariff.

As we said in our policy document *Britain is Working*, we have given the Royal Mail greater commercial freedom and have no plans to

21

privatise it. Our ambition is to see a publicly owned Royal Mail fully restored to good health, providing customers with an excellent service and its employees with rewarding employment. We will review the impact on the Royal Mail of market liberalisation, which is being progressively introduced under the Postal Services Act 2000 and which allows alternative carriers to the Royal Mail to offer postal services.

We have reformed our energy markets to make them open and competitive. And we are a leading force in the campaign to make Europe's energy markets the same. Our wider energy policy has created a framework that places the challenge of climate change – as well as the need to achieve security of supply – at the heart of our energy policy. We have a major programme to promote renewable energy, as part of a strategy of having a mix of energy sources from nuclear power stations to clean coal to micro-generators.

We will only regulate where necessary and will set exacting targets for reducing the costs of administering regulations. We will rationalise business inspections. The merger of the Inland Revenue and Customs and Excise will cut the administrative costs of tax compliance for small businesses.

We will take further action in Europe to ensure that EU regulations are proportionate and better designed. We strongly support the creation of an EU single market in services to match the single market in goods – and want an effective directive to provide real benefits to consumers and new opportunities to British business. We will protect our employment standards. In developing the directive we will want to avoid any undermining of our regulatory framework.

We will continue to work to protect the rights of consumers, bringing forward proposals to strengthen and streamline consumer advocacy. We look forward to action from the banking industry to remove delays in processing cheques and other payments and, if necessary, will legislate to ensure this early in the next Parliament.

There are many bank accounts that are lying dormant and unclaimed, often because people have forgotten about them or because the owner has died. We will work with the financial services industry to establish a common definition and a comprehensive record of unclaimed assets. We will then expect banks, over the course of the Parliament, to either reunite those assets with their owners or to channel them back into the community.

An effective planning regime protects the environment while promoting economic growth – and does so quickly and responsively. In the next term, we will ensure that our planning system continues to protect the sustainability of local and regional environments – and we will continue to develop a regime which is simpler, faster and more responsive to local and business needs including the need to create jobs and regenerate our cities.

■ Fostering entrepreneurship

There are 300,000 more businesses now than in 1997. We are tackling barriers to financing for small and growing businesses – especially enterprises in deprived areas. Through Business Links we will offer start-ups, social enterprises and small businesses access to tailored intensive support and coaching. To foster the entrepreneurs of tomorrow, by 2006 every school in the country will offer enterprise education, and every college and university should be twinned with a business champion.

■ Modern transport infrastructure

An efficient transport system is vital to the country's future, to our economy and to our quality of life. We welcome the freedom that additional travel provides and support the continuing development of a

23

competitive and efficient freight sector. Investment, better management of road and rail, and planning ahead are vital to deal with the pressures on the system in a way that respects our environmental objectives.

We have doubled transport spending since 1997 and will increase it year on year – committing over £180 billion in public money between now and 2015 as well as private investment. The Eddington Review will work with the Government to advise on how this investment should be targeted – in particular, where transport is vital to underpin economic growth.

We are now taking charge of setting the strategy for rail to further raise the standard of service and reliability. We will examine options for increasing capacity, including a new generation of high-speed trains on intercity routes and a new life for rural branch lines as community railways. We are committed to continuing to work to develop a funding and finance solution for the Crossrail project; and will look at the feasibility and affordability of a new North-South high-speed link.

We will support light-rail improvements where they represent value for money and are part of the best integrated transport solution. To that end, we are working with cities across the country and have committed £520 million to Manchester for Metrolink. We will support the continuing upgrade of the London Underground and the extension of the East London line.

Major investment is planned to expand capacity on the M1, M6 and M25. We must also manage road space better. We are examining the potential benefits of a parallel Expressway on the M6 corridor. We will introduce car-pool lanes for cars with more than one passenger on suitable roads and explore other ways to lock in the benefit of new capacity. We will complete the introduction of Traffic Management Officers to keep traffic flowing. Because of the long-term nature of transport planning, we will seek political consensus in tackling congestion, including examining the potential of moving away from the current system of motoring taxation towards a national system of road-pricing.

We will give all over-60s, and disabled people, free off-peak local bus travel and give local authorities the freedom to provide more generous schemes. We will continue to support growth in bus provision including innovation in school transport, with greater opportunity for local authorities to control their bus networks where they are demonstrating value for money and taking strong measures to tackle congestion. To facilitate improved public transport provision, we will explore giving Passenger Transport Executives greater powers over local transport.

We will continue funding local authorities and voluntary groups to make cycling and walking more attractive. We are committed to reducing child deaths and serious injuries on the road by 50 per cent, and we will continue to work to reduce dangerous driving, especially drink driving and uninsured driving. We will work with industry to make travel on public transport safer and more secure.

Government will continue to support technological innovation to reduce carbon emissions such as the hydrogen fuel-cell buses in London. We will explore the scope for further use of economic instruments as well as other measures to promote lower vehicle emissions.

We will continue to support air travel by implementing the balanced policies set out in our aviation white paper. We are committed to using the UK's 2005 presidency of the European Union to promote the inclusion of aviation in the EU's emissions trading scheme.

For shipping, our introduction of the tonnage tax has led to a trebling in size of the fleet since 1997. We want more ships to fly the British flag, to boost jobs and training, and to increase shipping and port capacity.

■ Opportunity for all

We are determined to spread the benefits of enterprise to every community in the country. Every regional economy has different strengths, and Regional Development Agencies now play an essential role in regional economic development.

'Our economy has grown in every quarter under this Government.'

We have given local authorities a direct incentive to promote local business creation, allowing them to keep up to £1 billion over three years of increased rate revenues to spend on their own priorities. The Local Enterprise Growth Initiative will work through local authorities to remove barriers to enterprise in the most deprived areas of England.

In 1997, many parts of our towns and cities were suffering from deeply entrenched and multiple disadvantage. To tackle this we established a ten-year programme, the New Deal for Communities, empowering local communities – and this is already delivering improvements in education outcomes and crime reduction.

No area in our country should be excluded from the opportunity to get ahead, to benefit from improving public services, and to be secure and safe. We will maintain our commitment to tackling issues of worklessness, low skills, crime, poor environment and health in our poorest neighbourhoods.

■ Fairness at work

Since 1997, the Labour Government has introduced new rights for people at work and new opportunities for trade unions to represent their members. We see modern, growing trade unions as an important part of our society and economy. They provide protection and advice for employees, and we welcome the positive role they have played in developing a modern model of social partnership with business representatives. The Labour Party has agreed a set of policies for the workplace (the Warwick Agreement) and we will deliver them in full. They will be good for employees and for the economy.

We have introduced, for the first time, an entitlement for every employee to four weeks' paid holiday, and we propose to extend this by making it additional to bank holiday entitlement.

■ Promoting equality at work

A strong economy draws on the talents of all. We have extended legislation to protect people from discrimination at work to cover not only gender, disability, race and ethnicity but also religion and sexual orientation and – from 2006 – age. Labour has transformed legal rights for disabled people. We will empower disabled people further by joining up services and expanding personalised budgets.

We will take further action to narrow the pay and promotion gap between men and women. The Women and Work Commission will report to the Prime Minister later this year.

We will implement the National Employment Panel's report on measures to promote employment and small business growth for ethnic and faith minorities. We will take forward the Strategy for Race Equality to ensure that we combat discrimination on the grounds of race and ethnicity across a range of services. The Equalities Review reporting to the Prime Minister in 2006 will make practical recommendations on the priorities for tackling disadvantage and promoting equality of opportunity for all groups.

■ Thriving rural areas

Since 1997, Labour has made it more difficult to close rural schools, put in £750 million to support rural post offices and introduced a 50 per cent rate relief on village shops. Through our £51 million Rural Bus Subsidy Grant we have delivered over 2,200 new bus services in rural areas this year.

We set targets for the creation of affordable homes in rural areas, which we have now exceeded. We will explore how to ensure a proportion of all new housing development is made available and affordable to local residents and their families.

Because of our success in achieving extensive reforms in the Common Agricultural Policy (CAP), 2005 will be the first year for decades when farmers will be free to produce for the market and not simply for subsidy. We will continue to push for further reform of the CAP in the next Parliament, starting with the sugar regime.

We will continue to promote the competitiveness of the whole food sector, and assure the safety and quality of its products. We will introduce an explicit policy for schools, hospitals and government offices to consider local sourcing of fresh produce. We will continue to improve the environmental performance of agriculture, rewarding every farmer in England for environmental protection and enhancement work through our new Stewardship schemes. We will also promote biomass, bio-fuels and non-food crops. We will work to tackle diffuse water pollution through addressing impacts across water catchments without the costs falling on water customers.

Under difficult circumstances, Labour is working with the fishing industry to create a sustainable long-term future for the fishing communities of the United Kingdom. We have reformed the Common Fisheries Policy and will continue to protect the marine environment and ensure fish stocks and their exploitation are set at sustainable levels.

We will introduce the Animal Welfare Bill as soon as possible in the new Parliament.

The choice for 2010

The Conservatives are the party of high interest rates, high inflation, mass unemployment and house repossessions. Their tax-and-spend promises do not add up; and they would cut £35 billion from public investment. With new Labour, Britain can seize the opportunities of globalisation, creating jobs and prosperity for people up and down the country. We can only do so if we build a clear sense of shared national economic purpose, not just around economic stability but also investment in infrastructure, skills, science and enterprise. The choice is to go forward to economic stability, rising prosperity and wider opportunities with new Labour. Or go back to the bad old days of Tory cuts, insecurity and instability.

Chapter 2

Education: More children making the grade
Forward to personalised learning, not back to mass failure

1997: 42nd in the World Education League

2005: Third best in the world for literacy at age ten and fastest improving for maths

2010: Every 16-year-old offered school, college, training or apprenticeship

Education is still our number one priority. In our first term, we transformed recruitment, training and methods of teaching, with record results in primary schools. In our second term we have driven fundamental reform in secondary provision – more teachers and support staff, more money, specialist schools and the Academies programmes. Our plan now is to tailor our education system to individual pupil needs, with parents supporting teachers and support staff in further raising standards. That means music, art, sport and languages as well as English and maths in primary school; a good secondary school for every child, with modern buildings and excellent specialist teaching; catch-up support for all children who need it; the guarantee of a sixth-form place, apprenticeship or further education at 16; sufficient quality and quantity in higher education. At each stage we send a clear message – every child has a right to a good education, but no child has the right to disrupt the education of other children.

■ The new Labour case

For generations our country has been held back by an education system that excelled for the privileged few but let down the majority. Every child can and should be able to fulfil their potential. We will achieve this by uniting our commitment to equal opportunities for all children with a reform programme which gives every child and young person, from pre-school to sixth-form or apprenticeship and beyond, the personalised package of learning and support they need. In a third term, we will entrench high expectations for every child, ensure the flexibility of provision to meet all needs and make parents true partners as we aim for the highest ever school standards.

■ Every pupil with better teaching

There is no greater responsibility than teaching the next generation. Head teachers, teachers and support staff deserve support and

'Our plan now is to tailor our education system to individual pupil needs, with parents supporting teachers and support staff in further raising standards.'

respect. There are now over 28,000 more teachers and 105,000 more support staff than in 1997; graduate teacher applications are up 70 per cent; average salaries are up by more than 30 per cent. The remodelling of the school workforce is benefiting staff and helping to tailor provision to pupil need. We will now go further – to intensify in-service training for teachers, to widen further routes into teaching, to help more teachers and pupils get the benefit of the range of support staff now working in schools, from learning mentors to music and arts specialists. The goal is clear: every pupil with extra support in their weakest subjects and extra opportunities in their strongest.

We want to see every pupil mastering the basics. If they are not mastered by 11, there will be extra time in the secondary curriculum to get them right: schools will be judged on how pupils do in English and maths at the ages of 11, 14 and 16.

We want every pupil to be stretched, including the brightest, so we will develop extended projects at A-level, harder A-level questions to challenge the most able, and give universities the individual module marks – as well as overall grades – of A-level students.

■ Every school with more money and effective leadership

Since 1997, school funding has risen by £1,000 per pupil. Education spending that was 4.7 per cent of national income in 1997 will rise to 5.5 per cent this year. We will continue to raise the share of national income devoted to education. And we will continue to recognise the additional needs of disadvantaged pupils. We will also ensure fundamental reform in the way the money is spent. Funding will be allocated on a multi-year timescale. There will be a dedicated national schools budget set by central government, with a guaranteed per pupil increase for every school. Heads and governors will be in control. Successful schools and colleges will have the independence to take decisions about how to deploy resources and develop their provision. Schools will work together to raise standards. New provision will be created where standards are too low or innovation is needed. Local authorities have a vital role in championing the parent interest and providing support services.

A strong, effective governing body is essential to the success of every school and governors must be given support to help them play this role. We will allow more flexibility in the structure of governing bodies, including the ability to have smaller governing bodies, of ten members or less, to streamline management while strengthening the position of parents.

■ Parents as partners

Our aim for the education system is to nurture the unique talents of every child. But children and schools do best with real and effective parental engagement. Parents should have the information and support they need to encourage their children, from the first reading book to the key choices they make at 14 and 16. And parents should be central to the process of assessing school performance and driving improvement, as well as their vital role in promoting good behaviour and raising the quality of school meals (see chapter 4).

All schools should have good home-school links, building on the new school and pupil profiles. Some schools are using ICT to make contact between parents and schools easier and better for both sides. We will encourage all schools to follow suit.

Ofsted now actively seeks the views of parents when undertaking inspections. Ofsted will be given new powers to respond to parental complaints and where necessary to close failing schools or replace failing management.

■ Enriching primary schools

International studies show that our ten-year-olds are the third highest achievers in literacy in the world and the fastest improving in maths. Three-quarters of 11-year-olds now reach high standards in reading, writing and maths. We will intensify our literacy and numeracy programme to help an extra 50,000 pupils achieve high standards at age 11, reaching our targets of 85 per cent of pupils succeeding at the basics.

All primary school children will have access to high-quality tuition in the arts, music, sport and foreign languages. We have set aside funds for this purpose, working with head teachers to develop support programmes and modernise the school workforce.

We have abolished infant class sizes of more than 30, and almost all primary schools have gained improved facilities since 1997. We will now upgrade primary schools nationwide in a 15-year Building Schools for the Future programme, including under-fives and childcare facilities where needed. Primary schools will become the base for a massive expansion of out-of-school provision (see chapter 6).

Foundation schools operate within the local family of state schools, and are funded in the same way as others, but manage their own assets and employ their staff directly. We will allow successful primary schools, like secondary schools, to become foundation schools by a simple vote of their governing body following consultation with their parents.

■ Every secondary school an independent specialist school

We want all secondary schools to be independent specialist schools with a strong ethos, high-quality leadership, good discipline (including school uniforms), setting by ability and high-quality facilities as the norm.

The way to achieve this is not a return to the 11-plus or a free-for-all on admissions policies. It is to ensure that independent specialist

'...we will entrench high expectations for every child, provide the flexibility of provision to meet all needs and make parents true partners as we aim for the highest ever school standards.'

schools tailor education to the needs, interests and aptitudes of each pupil within a fair admissions system.

There are over 2,000 specialist schools – schools which teach the entire national curriculum and also have a centre of excellence. Their results are improving faster than those of non-specialist schools. We want every secondary school to become a specialist school and existing specialist schools will be able to take on a second specialism. Over time all specialist schools will become extended schools, with full programmes of after-school activities.

Every part of the country will benefit, over fifteen years, from the Building Schools for the Future programme. This is a once in a generation programme to equip the whole country with modern secondary education facilities, open five days a week, ten hours a day.

Good schools will be able to expand their size and also their influence – by taking over less successful schools. We will develop a system to create rights for successful schools to establish sixth-form provision where there is pupil and parent demand, extending quality and choice for local students.

Britain has a positive tradition of independent providers within the state system, including church and other faith schools. Where new educational providers can help boost standards and opportunities in a locality we will welcome them into the state system, subject to parental demand, fair funding and fair admissions.

We strongly support the new Academies movement. Seventeen of these independent non-selective schools are now open within the state system; their results are improving sharply, and 50 more are in the pipeline. Within the existing allocation of resources our aim is that at least 200 Academies will be established by 2010 in communities where low aspirations and low performance are entrenched.

We will encourage more small schools and boarding schools as ways of helping the most disadvantaged children. We will make sure schools in deprived areas receive the resources they need. To enable all young people to enjoy the opportunities previously enjoyed by the few, we are developing a nationwide week-long summer residential programme for school students. We support partnership between the state and private sectors to bridge the unhealthy historic divide between the two.

■ Good discipline

Every pupil has the right to learn without disruption; no teacher should be subject to abuse or disrespect. We have given head teachers the powers needed to maintain discipline and the highest standards of conduct. Violent behaviour, including the use of knives will not be tolerated. We are also working with schools and teacher organisations to implement a zero tolerance approach to lower-level disruption. The number of places in out-of-school units has almost doubled, and the quality of provision has been enhanced. We will give head teachers within each locality direct control of the budgets for out-of-school provision, so they can expand and improve it as needed. We will encourage more dedicated provision for disruptive and excluded pupils, including by charities and voluntary groups with expertise in this area, and no school will become a dumping ground for such pupils.

Parents have a duty to get their children to attend school. We have introduced parenting orders and fines and will continue to advocate truancy sweeps.

■ Special educational needs

Children with special educational needs require appropriate resources and support from trained staff. For some this will be in mainstream schools; for others, it will be in special schools. Parents should have access to the special education appropriate for their child. It is the role of local authorities to make decisions on the shape of local provision, in consultation with local parents.

No more dropping out at 16

The historic problems of our education system at 14-plus have been an academic track that has been too narrow and a vocational offer too weak.

We are determined to raise the status and quality of vocational education. Beyond the age of 14, GCSEs and A-levels will be the foundation of the system in which high-quality vocational programmes will be available to every pupil. Designed in collaboration with employers, specialised diplomas will be established in key areas of the economy, leading to apprenticeships, to further and higher education and to jobs with training. We will review progress on the development of the 14-19 curriculum in 2008.

We will not let economic disadvantage stand in the way of young people staying in education beyond the age of 16. We have rolled out Educational Maintenance Allowances, providing lower income students with a £30-a-week staying-on allowance. We believe that everyone up to the age of 19 should be learning, so we will expand sixth-form, college and apprenticeship places, and ensure that all 16- to 19-year-olds in employment get access to training.

We believe that every 16- to 19-year-old should have dedicated supervision and support, including in the further education sector. We will support sixth-form colleges and expect FE colleges to have dedicated centres for 16- to 19-year-olds.

Further education is vital to vocational lifelong learning. Achieving a transformation of FE colleges requires both our increased investment and serious reform. Every FE college will develop a centre for vocational excellence, and we will establish new skills academies led by leading entrepreneurs and employers from the relevant skill sectors. Sir Andrew Foster's review will help shape the reform process.

■ Children's Trusts

Ofsted reports show that local government is continuing to improve the vital services on which schools and families rely. Education and social services should collaborate to help youngsters, especially the most vulnerable, achieve their potential. Local government should be the champion of parents and high-quality provision, including special needs education, school transport, and other support services. We are reforming local education authorities to form Children's Trusts to provide seamless support to children and families and work in partnership with the private and voluntary sectors.

■ World-class higher education, open to all

Universities are critical to Britain's future prosperity. We need a bigger, better higher education system. We are investing £1 billion more in the science base, and increasing public spending on higher education by 34 per cent in real terms. But graduates and employers must also play their part. Our funding reforms will generate £1 billion of extra funds by 2010; the abolition of up-front fees and the creation of grants will help poorer students. A quarter of the income from the new student finance system will go to bursaries for students from poorer families. The maximum annual fee paid by students will not rise above £3,000 (uprated annually for inflation) during the next Parliament.

As school standards rise we maintain our aim for 50 per cent of young people to go on to higher education by 2010. Two-year foundation degrees in vocational disciplines have a key part to play.

PhD students are vital to universities and the nation's research base.

The number of PhD students in the UK has risen by nearly 10,000 since 1997, and we are carrying through a 30 per cent increase in average PhD stipends to make doctoral research still more attractive to high-flyers.

We will incentivise all universities to raise more charitable and private funding for student bursaries and endowments.

The choice for 2010

Under their last government the Conservatives spent more on unemployment and debt interest than on education. Their priority now is to take at least £1 billion from state schools to subsidise private education for the privileged few. In addition they would allow a free-for-all in school admissions – including an extension of selection – for five- and 11-year-olds, cap the number of pupils who can succeed at GCSE and A-level, and reduce places in higher education. The choice for 2010 is forward with new Labour: pupils with quality and opportunity through the system from three to 18; parents with the confidence that where there is no improvement there will be intervention; teachers knowing that quality will be supported and rewarded; and employers with a system that gets the basics right and provides the skills that industry needs. Or back with the Tories to an education system designed to look after the few but fail the many.

Chapter 3

Crime and security:
Safe communities, secure borders
Forward to neighbourhood policing, not back to rising crime

1979-1997:	Recorded crime had almost doubled
2005:	Almost 13,000 more police officers
2010:	A neighbourhood policing team in every community

Today, there is less chance of being a victim of crime than for more than 20 years. But our security is threatened by major organised crime; volume crimes such as burglary and car theft, often linked to drug abuse; fear of violent crime; and anti-social behaviour. Each needs a very different approach. We are giving the police and local councils the power to tackle anti-social behaviour; we will develop neighbourhood policing for every community and crack down on drug dealing and hard drug use to reduce volume crime; we are modernising our asylum and immigration system; and we will take the necessary measures to protect our country from international terrorism.

■ The new Labour case

The modern world offers freedoms and opportunities unheralded a generation ago. But with new freedoms come new fears and threats to our security. Our progressive case is that to counter these threats we need strong communities built on mutual respect and the rule of law. We prize the liberty of the individual; but that means protecting the law-abiding majority from the minority who abuse the system. We believe in being tough on crime and its causes so we will expand drugs testing and treatment, and tackle the conditions – from lack of youth provision to irresponsible drinking – that foster crime and anti-social behaviour. In a third term we will make the contract of rights and responsibilities an enduring foundation of community life.

■ A neighbourhood policing team for every community

Overall crime as measured by the authoritative British Crime Survey is down 30 per cent – the equivalent of almost five million fewer crimes a year. Record numbers of police – almost 13,000 more than in 1997 – working with 4,600 new Community Support Officers (CSOs), local councils, and the Crown Prosecution Service deserve the credit. But local people want a more visible police presence and a role in setting local police priorities. So our pledge is a neighbourhood policing team for every community. We will carry on funding the police service to enable it to continue to employ historically high numbers of police officers.

Hard-working police officers should be supported by professional and trained support staff. So a new £340 million a year fund will take CSO numbers up to 24,000 – to work alongside the equivalent of an additional 12,000 police officers freed up for frontline duties. And we will work with representatives of police officers and other police staff to develop a modern career framework for the whole police team.

Not all problems need a 999 response, so a single phone number staffed by police, local councils and other local services will be available across the country to deal with anti-social behaviour and other non-emergency problems.

■ Empowering communities against anti-social behaviour

People want communities where the decent law-abiding majority are in charge. The experience of almost 4,000 Anti-Social Behaviour Orders, nearly 66,000 Penalty Notices for Disorder, and the closure of over 150 crack houses shows that communities can fight back against crime. We are ready to go further.

Parish Council wardens, like those working for local authorities, will be given the power to issue Penalty Notices for Disorder for noise, graffiti and throwing fireworks. Victims of anti-social behaviour will be able to give evidence anonymously. Local people will be able to take on 'neighbours from hell' by triggering action by councils and the police.

We have reformed housing and planning legislation to ensure that councils plan for the needs of genuine Gypsies and travellers. But with rights must go responsibilities so we have provided tough new powers

'We are giving the police and local councils the power to tackle anti-social behaviour; we will develop neighbourhood policing for every community…'

for councils and the police to tackle the problem of unauthorised sites.

Excessive alcohol consumption fuels anti-social behaviour and violence. The new Licensing Act will make it easier for the police and councils to deal with pubs and clubs that cause problems. Local councils and police will be able to designate Alcohol Disorder Zones to help pay for extra policing around city centre pubs and clubs, with new powers to immediately shut down premises selling alcohol to underage drinkers, and bans from town and city centres for persistent offenders. Police will be able to exclude yobs from town centres for 24 hours when they issue a Penalty Notice for Disorder.

'We believe in being tough on crime and its causes so we will expand drugs testing and treatment, and tackle the conditions…that foster crime and anti-social behaviour.'

We will continue to overhaul our youth justice system and improve Young Offender Institutions. We will make more use of intensive community programmes, including electronic tagging and tracking to deal with the most persistent young offenders, and will increase the number of parents of young offenders getting help with their children's behaviour. We will increase, by at least a half, programmes targeted at young people most at risk of offending and will expand drug-treatment services for young people.

■ Cutting crime through cutting drug dependency

Communities know that crime reduction depends on drug reduction. There are now 54 per cent more drug users in treatment and new powers for the police to close crack houses and get drug dealers off our streets. We will introduce compulsory drug testing at arrest for all property and drugs offenders, beginning in high-crime areas, with compulsory treatment assessment for those who test positive. Offenders under probation supervision will be randomly drug tested to mirror what already happens to offenders in custody.

From 2006, the Serious Organised Crime Agency will bring together over 4,000 specialist staff to tackle terrorism, drug dealers, people traffickers and other national and international organized criminals. And in consultation with local police authorities and chief constables we will re-structure police resources in order to develop strong leadership, streamline all police support services, and focus upon national and regional organised crime.

■ Reducing the use of guns and knives

Dangerous weapons fuel violence. We have banned all handguns, introduced five-year minimum sentences for those caught with an unlawful firearm and raised the age limit for owning an air gun. Now we will go further. We will introduce a Violent Crime Reduction Bill to restrict the sale of replica guns, raise the age limit for buying knives to 18 and tighten the law on air guns. Head teachers will have legal rights to search pupils for knives or guns. At-risk pubs and clubs will be required to search for them and we will introduce tougher sentences for carrying replica guns, for those involved in serious knife crimes and for those convicted of assaulting workers serving the public.

■ Punishing criminals, reducing offending

As court sentences have got tougher, we have built over 16,000 more prison places than there were in 1997. The most high-risk violent offenders will now be detained in custody indefinitely and our 2003 Criminal Justice Act confirmed that life sentences must mean life for the most heinous murders. Where significant new evidence comes to light we have abolished the 'double jeopardy' rule so that serious criminals who have been unjustly acquitted can be tried again. And we will introduce much tougher penalties for those who cause death by careless driving or who kill while driving without a licence or while disqualified.

We will tackle reoffending. By 2007 every offender will be supervised after release; we will increase the use of electronic tagging; and we will test the use of compulsory lie detector tests to monitor convicted sex offenders. Our new National Offender Management Service will ensure that every offender is individually case-managed from beginning to end of their sentence, both in and out of custody – with increased effort targeted on drugs treatment, education and basic skills training to reduce reoffending. Voluntary organisations and the private sector will be offered greater opportunities to deliver offender services and we will give local people a greater say in shaping community punishment.

■ Making sure crime does not pay

Those who commit crimes should not profit from them. Already we have introduced laws that enable the courts to confiscate the assets and property of drug dealers and other major criminals. We will enable the police and prosecuting authorities to keep at least half of all the criminal assets they seize to fund local crime-fighting priorities. And we will develop new proposals to ensure that criminals are not able to profit from publishing books about their crimes. In addition we will support magistrates effectively in fighting crime and improve the enforcement of court decisions – including the payment of fines.

Where a defendant fails to turn up for court without good excuse, the presumption should be that the trial and sentencing should go ahead anyway.

We will overhaul laws on fraud and the way that fraud trials are conducted to update them for the 21st century and make them quicker and more effective.

'Overall crime…is down 30 per cent – the equivalent of almost five million fewer crimes a year.'

■ Backing the victim

The legal system must dispense justice to the victim as well as the accused. We have invested to create a modern, self-confident prosecution service. With new powers and new technology to bring more offenders to justice more speedily and effectively. We will improve the way the courts work for victims, witnesses and jurors by:

* *Building a nationwide network of witness and victim support units that provide practical help.*
* *Expanding specialist courts to deal with domestic violence and specialist advocates to support the victims of such crime and of other serious crimes like murder and rape.*

We will extend the use of restorative justice schemes and Community Justice Centres to address the needs of victims, resolve disputes and help offenders to make recompense to victims for their crimes.

Legal aid will be reformed to better help the vulnerable. We will ensure independent regulation of the legal profession, and greater competition in the legal services market to ensure people get value for money. We will tackle the compensation culture – resisting invalid claims, but upholding people's rights.

'We prize the liberty of the individual; but that means protecting the law-abiding majority from the minority who abuse the system.'

Following consultation on the draft Bill we have published, we will legislate for a new offence of corporate manslaughter.

■ Migration: The facts

Over seven million people entered the UK from outside the EU in 2003: of whom 180,000 came here to work and over 300,000 to study, with the rest coming here as business visitors and tourists. People from overseas spent almost £12 billion in the UK, and overseas students alone are worth £5 billion a year to our economy. At a time when we have over 600,000 vacancies in the UK job market, skilled migrants are contributing 10-15 per cent of our economy's overall growth.

Since 1997, the time taken to process an initial asylum application has been reduced from 20 months to two months in over 80 per cent of cases. The number of asylum applications has been cut by two-thirds since 2002. The backlog of claims has been cut from over 50,000 at the end of 1996 to just over 10,000. There are 550 UK Immigration Officers posted in France and Belgium to check passports of people boarding boats and trains, and Airline Liaison Officers and overseas entry clearance staff are helping to stop 1,000 people a day improperly entering the UK.

■ Building a strong and diverse country

For centuries Britain has been a home for people from the rest of Europe and further afield. Immigration has been good for Britain. We want to keep it that way.

Our philosophy is simple: if you are ready to work hard and there is work for you to do, then you are welcome here. We need controls that work and a crackdown on abuse to ensure that we have a robust and fair immigration system fit for the 21st century that is in the interests of Britain.

■ A points system for immigration

We need skilled workers. So we will establish a points system for those seeking to migrate here. More skills mean more points and more chance of being allowed to come here.

We will ensure that only skilled workers are allowed to settle long-term in the UK, with English language tests for everyone who wants to stay permanently and an end to chain migration.

Where there has been evidence of abuse from particular countries, the immigration service will be able to ask for financial bonds to guarantee that migrants return home. We will continue to improve the quality and speed of immigration and asylum decisions. Appeal rights for non-family immigration cases will be removed and we will introduce civil penalties on employers of up to £2,000 for each illegal immigrant they employ.

■ Strong and secure borders

While the Tories would halve investment in our immigration services, we would invest in the latest technology to keep our borders strong and secure.

By 2008, those needing a visa to enter the UK will be fingerprinted. We will issue ID cards to all visitors planning to stay for more than three months. Over the next five years we will implement a new electronic borders system that will track visitors entering or leaving the UK.

Across the world there is a drive to increase the security of identity documents and we cannot be left behind. From next year we are introducing biometric 'ePassports'. It makes sense to provide citizens with an equally secure identity card to protect them at home from identity theft and clamp down on illegal working and fraudulent use of public services. We will introduce ID cards, including biometric data like fingerprints, backed up by a national register and rolling out initially on a voluntary basis as people renew their passports.

■ Fair rules

We can and should honour our obligations to victims of persecution without allowing abuse of the asylum system. We will:

* *Fast-track all unfounded asylum seekers with electronic tagging where necessary and more use of detention as we expand the number of detention places available.*
* *Remove more failed applicants. We have more than doubled the number of failed asylum seekers we remove from the UK compared to 1996. By fingerprinting every visa applicant and prosecuting those who deliberately destroy their documents we will speed up the time taken to redocument and remove people and will take action against those countries that refuse to cooperate. By the end of 2005, our aim is for removals of failed asylum seekers to exceed new unfounded claims.*

■ Tough action to combat international terrorism

We know that there are people already in the country and who seek to enter the United Kingdom who want to attack our way of life. Our liberties are prized but so is our security.

Police and other law enforcement agencies now have the powers they need to ban terrorist organisations, to clampdown on their fundraising and to hold suspects for extended questioning while charges are brought. Over 700 arrests have been made since 2001. Wherever possible, suspects should be prosecuted through the courts in the normal way. So we will introduce new laws to help catch and convict those involved in helping to plan terrorist activity or who glorify or condone acts of terror. But we also need to disrupt and prevent terrorist activity. New control orders will enable police and security agencies to keep track on those they suspect of planning terrorist outrages including bans on who they can contact or meet, electronic tagging and curfew orders, and for those who present the highest risk, a requirement to stay permanently at home.

We will continue to improve coordination between enforcement agencies and cooperation with other countries so that every effort is made to defeat the terrorists.

The choice for 2010

Labour's goals for 2010 are clear. Overall crime down, the number of offenders brought to justice up, with a neighbourhood policing team in every community to crack down on crime and disorder and a modern criminal justice system fit for the 21st century. And to reduce threats from overseas: secure borders backed up by ID cards and a crackdown on abuse of our immigration system. The Conservative threat is equally clear. Savage cuts to our border controls, 'fantasy island' asylum policies and a return to the days of broken promises on police numbers and crime investment.

'We will introduce ID cards, including biometric data like fingerprints, backed up by a national register and rolling out initially on a voluntary basis as people renew their passports.'

Britain
forward
not back

Chapter 4

Our NHS: Free to all, personal to each
Forward to personalised healthcare
for all of us, not back to two-tier
healthcare

1997: 12-hour waits in Accident and Emergency,
      and waiting more than 18 months for
      operations

2005: Less than four hours in A&E for 97 per
      cent of patients. Virtually no one waiting
      more than nine months for an operation

2008: No one waiting more than 18 weeks from
      referral to treatment. No hidden waits.
      Free choice of hospital

The NHS is being restored to good health: more doctors, more nurses, better facilities. Waiting times are coming down and the survival rates for the biggest killers are improving. The revolution in quantity of care must be matched by a revolution in quality of care. With equal access for all and no charges for operations. That means new types of health provision, more say for patients in how, where and when they are treated, and tackling ill-health at source.

■ The new Labour case

Healthcare is too precious to be left to chance, too central to life chances to be left to your wealth. Access to treatment should be based on your clinical need not on your ability to pay. This means defeating those who would dismantle the NHS. But it also means fundamentally reforming the NHS to meet new challenges – a more demanding citizenry with higher expectations, major advances in science and medical technology, changes in the composition and needs of the population.

'We promised to revive the NHS; we have. In our third term we will make the NHS safe for a generation.'

So our aim is an NHS free to all of us and personal to each of us. We will deliver through high national standards backed by sustained investment, by using new providers where they add capacity or promote innovation, and most importantly by giving more power to patients over their own treatment and over their own health.

57

We promised to revive the NHS; we have. In our third term we will make the NHS safe for a generation.

■ New investment

NHS spending has doubled since 1997, and will triple by 2008; already we have an extra 27,000 doctors in post or in training and 79,000 extra nurses; over 100 new hospital building projects under way; 500,000 more operations a year. We are proud of the dedication and commitment of NHS staff. We have widened the responsibilities of nurses and pharmacists, paramedics and porters, creating health services more convenient for patients.

Together with our organisational reforms, the investment is paying off. The maximum time that people waited for operations in 1997 was well over 18 months. Now virtually no one waits longer than nine months, and this year it will fall further to six months. For a heart operation or for cataract removal no one is waiting longer than three months; 97 per cent of people wait less than four hours in Accident and Emergency before treatment, admission or discharge. And speedier treatment saves lives. Death rates from heart disease are down by 27 per cent since 1996; from cancer by 12 per cent.

We will do even better. For too long waiting times have only counted the time after diagnosis. We will be the first Government to include all waiting times in this calculation, including waiting for outpatient appointments and for test results. There will be no hidden waits. So:

* *By the end of 2008, no NHS patient will have to wait longer than a maximum of 18 weeks from the time they are referred for a hospital operation by their GP until the time they have that operation. This would mean an average wait of nine to ten weeks.*
* *We will commit to faster test results for cervical smears.*
* *We will go further in improving cancer waiting times.*

'The NHS is being
restored to good health:
more doctors, more nurses,
better facilities…
The revolution in
quantity of care must
be matched by a revolution
in quality of care.'

All this with equal access for all, free at the point of need with no charges for hospital operations.

We have tightened the rules on NHS operations so that 'health tourists' now have to pay for treatment.

'One principle underpins our reforms –
putting patients centre stage.
And extending patient power and
choice is crucial to achieving this.'

We will deal with the challenge of MRSA. Infections acquired in hospital are not new. The time to destroy MRSA was in the early 1990s – when only five per cent of the bacteria were resistant to antibiotics. At that time the Tory government did not even keep records about the incidence of MRSA and were forcing hospitals to contract out cleaning services. We were the first government to publish statistics on the problem. Now, thanks to the tough measures we have already taken, including the end to a two-tier workforce for contracted-out cleaning services, MRSA rates are on their way down. But there is still some way to go. We all want clean hospitals, free of infection. We have already reintroduced hospital matrons and given them unprecedented powers to deal with cleanliness and infections in their wards; we shall reinforce this by consulting on new laws to enforce higher hygiene standards

And by strengthening accountability and cutting bureaucracy, we shall ensure that the new investment is not squandered. We are decreasing the numbers of staff in the Department of Health by a third, and are halving the numbers of quangos – freeing up £500 million for front-line staff. Given the pace of change within medical services we will ensure that it is possible for the NHS to change the way in which it organises its services as quickly as possible. Further streamlining measures will allow us to release an additional £250 million a year for front-line services by 2007.

In the light of the findings of the Shipman Inquiry, we will strengthen clinical governance in the NHS to ensure that professional activity is fully accountable to patients, their families and the wider public. Following the recommendation of the Health Select Committee, we will require registration of all clinical trials and publication of their findings for all trials of medicinal products with a marketing authorisation in the UK.

■ Innovation and reform

To achieve our goals we need to expand and develop different types of provision. We will put more money into the frontline, develop practice-based commissioning, and so ensure that family doctors have more power over their budgets. We will create more services in primary care. We will build on our family doctor service with more GPs delivering more advanced services more locally; new walk-in centres for commuters; specialised diagnostic and testing services; comprehensive out-of-hours services; high-street drop-in centres for chiropody, physiotherapy and check-ups. And we will continue to expand the role of nurses. These changes will result in more quality, convenience and care.

Expansion in NHS capacity will come both from within the National Health Service – where we will develop the NHS Foundation Trust model and the new freedom for GPs to expand provision – as well as from the independent and voluntary sector, where specialist services are available at NHS standards to meet NHS need.

'Healthcare is too precious to be left to chance, too central to life chances to be left to your wealth…This means defeating those who would dismantle the NHS.'

To help create an even greater range of provision and further improve convenience, we will over the next five years develop a new generation of modern NHS community hospitals. These state-of-the-art centres will provide diagnostics, day surgery and outpatients facilities closer to where people live and work.

We shall continue to encourage innovation and reform through the use of the independent sector to add capacity to, and drive contestability within, the NHS. We have already commissioned 460,000 operations from the independent sector, which will all be delivered free – with equal access for all based on need, not the ability to pay.

Whenever NHS patients need new capacity for their healthcare, we will ensure that it is provided from whatever source.

■ Empowering patients: choosing not waiting

One principle underpins our reforms – putting patients centre stage. And extending patient power and choice is crucial to achieving this. We shall be embedding both throughout the NHS. So:

* *By the end of 2008, patients whose GPs refer them for an operation will be able to choose from any hospital that can provide that operation to NHS medical and financial standards. There will be the choice of a convenient time and place for a non-urgent operation for example a location close to relatives.*

* *We will expand capacity and choice in primary care too. Where GPs' lists are full we will expand provision by encouraging entrepreneurial GPs and other providers to expand into that location.*

* *By 2009 all women will have choice over where and how they have their baby and what pain relief to use. We want every woman to be supported by the same midwife throughout her pregnancy. Support will be linked closely to other services that will be provided in Children's Centres.*

* *In order to increase choices for patients with cancer we will double the*

investment going into palliative care services, giving more people the choice to be treated at home.

By October 2005 we will have recruited more than 1,000 new NHS dentists and will have increased the number of dental school places by 25 per cent. We will undertake a fundamental review of the scope and resourcing of NHS dentistry.

We will provide more information and advice. Through NHS Direct, Health Direct, interactive TV, print media and the internet we will give more convenient access to much better information about health and health services, including the performance of doctors and hospitals.

■ Empowering patients:
long-term conditions and social care

We will promote the integration of health and social care at local level, so that older people and those with long-term conditions can retain their independence. We will continue to provide healthcare free in long-term care establishments, and provide the right framework for schemes such as equity release which make staying at home an attractive option. We will develop our policy of community matrons for those with severe conditions, helping to keep people out of hospital by providing better care at home.

*We will develop personalised budgets in social care where people can decide for themselves what they need and how it should be provided.

*We shall extend case-management for the 18 million people with long-term conditions. We will treble the investment in the Expert Patients Programme, and help many more patients take control of their own care plans.

* Almost a third of people attending GP surgeries have mental health problems and mental health occupies approximately one third of a GP's time. So we will continue to invest in and improve our services for people with mental health problems at primary and secondary levels, including

behavioural as well as drug therapies.

*We shall provide safeguards for the few people with long-term mental health problems who need compulsory treatment coupled with appropriate protection for the public. We shall also strengthen the system for protecting the public from offenders who have served their sentence but may still pose a threat because they have a serious psychopathic disorder.

■ Living healthier lives

People want to take responsibility for their own health outside the NHS as well as within it. They have the right to expect help from government. The killer diseases of the heart and the many forms of cancer are often the product of poor diet, lack of exercise and above all smoking. By 2010 we aim to reduce deaths from coronary heart disease and strokes by 40 per cent from 1997. And we want death rates from cancer to be cut by 20 per cent.

■ Healthy choices for children

We will start the drive for better health early – at school. We have already extended the provision of free fruit to all 4- to 6-year-olds at school. We will invest more in renovating and building new kitchens as well as investing an extra £210 million in school meals, guaranteeing that at least 50p per meal is spent on ingredients in primary schools, and at least 60p in secondary schools. We are introducing an independent School Food Trust, better training for dinner ladies and Ofsted inspection of healthy eating. We will legislate for tougher standards of nutrition for school meals and will encourage schools to teach more about healthy eating. We will ban certain products that are high in fat/salt content from school meals and ensure that fresh fruit and vegetables are part of every school meal. We will encourage secondary schools to keep pupils on the premises to ensure that they have a healthy meal. We will ensure that all school children have access to a school nurse.

■ Healthy choices for all

We will put in place a simple system of labelling to make it easier for busy shoppers to see at a glance how individual foods contribute to a healthy balanced diet. We will help parents by restricting further the advertising and promotion to children of those foods and drinks that are high in fat, salt and sugar.

We recognise that many people want smoke-free environments and need regulation to help them get this. We therefore intend to shift the balance significantly in their favour. We will legislate to ensure that all enclosed public places and workplaces other than licensed premises will be smoke-free. The legislation will ensure that all restaurants will be smoke-free; all pubs and bars preparing and serving food will be smoke-free; and other pubs and bars will be free to choose whether to allow smoking or to be smoke-free. In membership clubs the members will be free to choose whether to allow smoking or to be smoke-free. However, whatever the general status, to protect employees, smoking in the bar area will be prohibited everywhere.

These restrictions will be accompanied by an expansion of NHS smoking cessation services to encourage and support smokers to improve their own health by giving up smoking

Starting with the poorest areas of the country we will introduce health trainers to help people maintain their healthy choices. By 2010, through this activity we plan to reduce the health inequalities that exist between rich and poor.

All this will be free at the point of need.

The choice for 2010

Today's Conservatives want to do what not even Margaret Thatcher would countenance – introducing charges for hospital

operations so that those who can afford to pay thousands of pounds can push ahead of those who cannot. As well as ending the founding principle of the health service, this would take more than £1 billion out of the system to subsidise those who can afford to pay. For the rest of us, the Tories would abandon waiting-list targets and allow a return to the 18-month waits that were their NHS legacy. The choice is forward with new Labour to a health system with patients in the driving seat, free to all and personal to each of us. Or back with the Tories to longer waits, and to a health system where treatment depends not on your condition but on your bank balance.

Chapter 5
Older people: Secure today, prepared for the future
Forward to new opportunities in old age, not back to poverty and insecurity

1997: 2.8 million pensioners in poverty, the poorest living on £69 per week

2005: Minimum income for pensioners of £109 per week

2010: A long-term settlement for pensions

Our priority since 1997 has been to tackle pensioner poverty. Nearly two million pensioners have been lifted out of absolute poverty as a result of Labour's measures, which are now getting on average an extra £2,000 a year to the poorest third. Our priorities now are to build a national consensus for tomorrow's pensioners, combining public and private pension schemes to build security in retirement, and to extend the quality of life of older people.

■ The new Labour case

By 2020 there will be more people over the age of 80 than under the age of five. For a progressive government there can be no compromise of our duty to today's pensioners. But while we fulfil that duty we must also see old age as a time of independence and opportunity. On pensions, our aim is a system that provides security and decency for all, which encourages and rewards saving, and is financially sustainable. And because, more than anything, people need certainty to plan for the future we will seek a national consensus – cross-party, cross-generation – for long-term reform.

■ Tackling pensioner poverty:
The success of the Pension Credit

In 1997, 2.8 million pensioners were living in poverty – with the poorest expected to live on just £69 per week. Labour's Pension Credit now means that no pensioner need live on less than £109 per week. It rewards saving and helps over three million pensioners, with women in particular benefiting. We will increase Pension Credit in line with earnings up to and including 2007-08.

All pensioners have benefited from improved universal benefits like the state pension, the Winter Fuel Payment (now worth £300 per year for the over-80s), help with council tax and free TV licences for the over-75s. This year, all households expected to pay council tax that

'On pensions, our aim is a system that provides security and decency for all, which encourages and rewards saving, and is financially sustainable.'

include anyone over 65 will receive £200 towards the cost of council tax, and the following year there will be free, off-peak local bus travel in England for the over-60s.

Millions of pensioners have benefited from our fuel poverty programme. Our goal is to eliminate fuel poverty for vulnerable groups by 2010, and for all by 2015.

■ Pensions for the generation of tomorrow

The generation retiring in the future will be different in many ways from its predecessors. Their jobs will have been different; the expectations of women will be transformed; their retirements will be longer and healthier. We have begun to lay the foundations for the pensions system of tomorrow, for example, by: introducing the State Second Pension to ensure carers, low earners and disabled people have a chance to build up a decent pension for the first time; encouraging automatic enrolment into company pension schemes; creating the Pension Protection Fund; enabling pensioners for the first time to work part time and draw down their occupational pension; as well as offering an increased state pension or lump sum for those deferring their pension. We will work to increase the proportion of pension fund trustees nominated by scheme members, along with access to proper training. We will keep this issue under review, with consultation in the expectation of further progress to 50 per cent member-nominated trustees.

We need to forge a national consensus about how we move from a pension system designed for today's pension problems to one that is right for tomorrow's. We appointed the Pensions Commission to look into the future of pensions and its second report is due in autumn 2005. We are clear about the goals of a reformed system. It must tackle poverty, provide everyone with the opportunity to build an adequate retirement income, and be affordable, fair and simple to understand. In particular it must address the disadvantages faced by women.

■ New rights, new choices

Many older people want to carry on working in their 50s and 60s. The welfare state should be there to help them. Older people with their skills and experience are potentially an enormous resource. That is why we set up the New Deal for the Over-50s, with over 150,000 older people helped back to work.

We also need to put the force of the law on the side of older people who wish to continue working. Companies will no longer be able to force people to retire before the age of 65 except where specifically justified. All employees over the age of 65 will have the right to request of their employer that they be allowed to carry on working. After five years we will review whether there should be any fixed retirement ages.

'…provide everyone with the opportunity to build an adequate retirement income, and be affordable, fair and simple to understand.'

We will give older people greater choice over their care. For every older person receiving care or other support, we want to offer transparent, individual budgets which bring funding for a range of services, including social care, care homes, and housing support such as adaptations, maintenance and cleaners together in one place. We will pilot individual budgets for older people by the end of this year.

We will make the most of the opportunities of an older population by creating a new programme for older people to be mentors and coaches to gifted and talented young people. We will also work with voluntary organisations to help expand grandparent and toddler groups across the country.

■ Support across the generations

The challenge of balancing work and family applies to parents but also to people looking after an elderly or sick relative – now one in five adults. Since the introduction of the right to request from their employer flexible working arrangements, a million parents have changed their working hours. We are consulting on a similar right for carers of elderly or sick relatives.

The choice for 2010

The Tories are the party of pensioner poverty. When they left office in 1997, one in four pensioners was living in poverty and the poorest pensioners were expected to get by on just £69 a week. They would phase out the Pension Credit and abolish the State Second Pension, hurting most those most in need. When the one thing we all need is certainty, the Tories have admitted they have absolutely no plans for how to fund their pensions policy beyond four years. The choice is whether we go forward with new Labour with today's pensioners provided for and poverty falling, a national consensus on fair and sustainable long-term reform and the policies to give older people enhanced rights and choices. Or back with the Tories to rising levels of pensioner poverty and unending insecurity for tomorrow's pensioners.

Chapter 6

Families: Choice and support at work and at home
Forward to family prosperity, not back to family poverty

1997: Childcare places for only one in eight children under eight

2005: Universal, free, part-time nursery education for all three- and four-year-olds

2010: Universal, affordable childcare for three- to 14-year-olds and a Sure Start Children's Centre in every community

It is impossible to fulfil the potential of our country – never mind promoting social mobility and equality of life chances – unless every child gets the best possible start in life. Government does not bring up children, but it must support parents in their key role. We will help parents balance work and family, expand paid leave, deliver the biggest ever expansion in childcare and end child poverty in a generation.

■ The new Labour case

Strong families are the bedrock of a strong society. Children cannot be the forgotten constituency of politics; parents put their children first and they deserve support from government. Yet fear of seeming to 'nanny' has in the past meant British law and culture have not supported parents and children. Government cannot shirk its responsibilities. Our starting point is that for children to come first parents need to be given choices: a tax and benefit system to raise family incomes and tackle child poverty; legal changes to promote a healthy balance between work and family; and services built around the needs of children. Our third-term commitment – not a nanny state but a family-friendly government.

■ Tackling child poverty

We will end child poverty, starting by halving it – both in terms of relative low-income and in terms of material deprivation – by 2010-11.

Work is the best anti-poverty strategy. Tailored help, especially for lone parents, is key but we are also committed to making work pay – with a guaranteed income of at least £258 per week for those with children and in full-time work.

The benefits system needs to support all children, and those in greatest need the most. That is the rationale for universal child benefit and targeted tax credits, and why we have committed to increasing the

75

Child Tax Credit at least in line with earnings up to and including 2007-08. By October 2005, families with children will be on average £1,400 per year better off, and those in the poorest fifth of the population on average £3,200 a year better off compared to 1997. Labour's Child Trust Fund creates a nest egg for newborns that they can access at age 18. It is the world's first example of a government ensuring that all children grow up with a financial stake. We are determined to see it grow and are consulting on making payments at age seven and at secondary school age, in addition to those made at birth.

'Over 350,000 mothers and 80,000 fathers each year are using new rights to paid maternity and paternity leave.'

We are supporting local authorities in the radical reform of children's services, above all to ensure there is one professional with lead responsibility for each vulnerable child. We will also ensure that services are designed to meet the additional needs of disabled children and their families.

■ Universal childcare

Since 1997, the Government has funded an additional 520,000 sustainable childcare places and now every family with a three- or four- year-old child has access to a free nursery place. By 2010, we will create 3,500 Sure Start Children's Centres for children under five years – five in every constituency – a universal local service that brings together childcare and services for families. By 2010, all parents of three- and four-year-olds will have increased rights to flexible, free, part-time nursery provision for 15 hours a week over the whole school year. Over the longer term we will increase free provision to 20 hours.

For older children up to the age of 14 extended schools, working in partnership with the private and voluntary sectors, will offer affordable out-of-school childcare from 8am to 6pm throughout the year, with a range of arts, music, sport and study support.

We will help families with incomes of up to £59,000 a year with their childcare costs through more generous Working Tax Credit, including help for those using a nanny or au pair. Parents using childcare supported by their employer will be able to get a tax break worth up to £50 a week each. We are working with the GLA and the Mayor to bring down the cost of childcare in London.

■ Creating time

Over 350,000 mothers and 80,000 fathers each year are using new rights to paid maternity and paternity leave. Parents consistently say their top priority is more choice of whether to stay at home with their baby in the first year of its life. We will therefore increase paid maternity leave to nine months from 2007 – worth an extra £1,400 – with the goal of achieving a year's paid leave by the end of the Parliament while simplifying the system for employers. We want to give fathers more opportunities to spend time with their children, and are consulting on how best to do this including the option of sharing paid leave. We have already introduced the right to request flexible working to parents of children under six and nearly a million parents have benefited. We need to balance the needs of parents and carers, with those of employers, especially small businesses. We are consulting on extending the right to request flexible working to carers of sick and disabled adults as a priority, and also on whether we should extend the right to parents of older children.

■ Supporting family life

Common sense, as well as research, says that children need to be able to depend on the love and support of both parents. The financial support we are giving families, along with new rights to flexible working and access to childcare, are all designed to support family life. Government can and should support those public and voluntary agencies that support families and parents. We are examining the development of a new information service – Parents Direct – to provide advice on all aspects of children's services and parental entitlements.

For those parents who do separate or divorce, both have a responsibility for a meaningful relationship with their children where that is safe. We are introducing reforms to minimise conflict and encourage conciliation by greater and early use of mediation. We stand by the principle that absent parents should make a fair contribution to the cost of the upkeep of their children, and we are committed to tackling the backlog of Child Support Agency claims as efficiently and fairly as possible. We also need to ensure court orders on access are enforced according to the best interests of the child, which ideally gives both parents an important role.

■ Increasing home ownership

A decent home is crucial to family well-being. Homeownership has increased by over one million with Labour and by the end of our third term we aim for it to have risen by another million to two million. Rising house prices in many areas of the country have made it difficult for people on lower incomes to get a foot on the housing ladder. So we have raised the stamp duty threshold from £60,000 to £120,000 for residential properties, exempting an extra 300,000 homebuyers from stamp duty every year.

We will continue to respond to the challenges of local housing markets across the UK. In the South we will invest in extra housing in London

'Children cannot be the forgotten constituency of politics; parents put their children first and they deserve support from government.'

and the wider South East, with particular emphasis on the Thames Gateway and other growth areas. In the Midlands and North we will tackle the problems of low demand and abandonment that threaten communities.

We want to widen the opportunity to own or part-own, especially for more young people and those tenants who rent in the private or public sector. Our comprehensive plan includes:

* *A new Homebuy scheme offering up to 300,000 council and housing association tenants the opportunity to buy part of their home, increasing their equity over time if they wish.*
* *A First Time Buyers Initiative to help over 15,000 first-time buyers who could not own or part-own a home without extra help. We will use surplus public land for new homes, enabling the buyer to take out a mortgage for only the building.*
* *Strengthening existing home ownership schemes, such as the Key Worker Living scheme and Shared Ownership.*

■ Social housing

The increased supply and quality of social housing is central to Labour's belief in mixed, sustainable communities.

Since 1997, we have cut the number of substandard social-rented homes by one million; installing 300,000 new kitchens, 220,000 new bathrooms and 720,000 new boilers and central heating systems into council homes. By 2010 we will ensure that all social tenants benefit from a decent, warm home with modern facilities.

For too long, tenants have had little say over where they live. In a third term, Labour will offer greater flexibility and choice for those who rent. We will increase the annual supply of new social homes by 50 per cent by 2008, an extra 10,000 homes a year, and give local authorities the ability to start building homes again and bring empty homes back into use. And we will end the 'take it or leave it' approach to social renting by expanding choice-based lettings nationwide.

The choice for 2010

The Tories are all talk and no action on family policy. They opposed our increases in maternity and paternity pay and the introduction of flexible working rights. Even the measures they have proposed wouldn't come in until 2009, by which time the Tories are committed to making deep cuts in spending. The choice is forward with new Labour to a universal, affordable, good-quality childcare, a million more homeowners, more choice for all parents and an end to child poverty. Or back to the risky economic policies of a Tory government that would let families sink or swim whatever the pressures they face.

Chapter 7

International policy: A stronger country in a secure, sustainable and just world

Forward to international leadership, not back to isolation and powerlessness

---

1997: Marginalised in Europe, aid in decline and Bosnia in ruins

2005: Aid doubled, elections in Iraq and Afghanistan, Kosovo and Bosnia peaceful

2010: A strong Britain in a reforming Europe, 300 million out of poverty, global action on climate change

Globalisation means that events elsewhere have a direct impact at home. So we will pursue British interests by working with our allies to make the world a safer, fairer place. This means reforming Europe. It means fighting terrorism and stopping the spread of weapons of mass destruction. It means modernising our armed forces. And it means using our leading role in the G8, EU, the Commonwealth and UN to promote global action on climate change and poverty.

■ The new Labour case

Domestic interests and international action are entwined more than ever before. Action on drugs, terrorism, people trafficking, AIDS, climate change, poverty, migration and trade all require us to work with other countries and through international organisations. The best defence of our security at home is the spread of liberty and justice overseas. In a third term we will secure Britain's place in the EU and at the heart of international decision-making. We will always uphold the rule of international law.

■ Making Europe work better for Britain

We are proud of Britain's EU membership and of the strong position Britain has achieved within Europe. British membership of the EU brings jobs, trade and prosperity; it boosts environmental standards, social protection and international clout. Since 1997 we have gone from marginal players, often ignored, to leaders in the European Union. Working hard with Labour MEPs, we are determined to remain leaders. Outside the EU, or on its margins, we would unquestionably be weaker and more vulnerable.

The EU now has 25 members and will continue to expand. The new Constitutional Treaty ensures the new Europe can work effectively, and that Britain keeps control of key national interests like foreign policy, taxation, social security and defence. The Treaty sets out what the

EU can do and what it cannot. It strengthens the voice of national parliaments and governments in EU affairs. It is a good treaty for Britain and for the new Europe. We will put it to the British people in a referendum and campaign whole-heartedly for a 'Yes' vote to keep Britain a leading nation in Europe.

We will also work to reform Europe. During Britain's EU presidency this year, we will work to promote economic reform, bear down on regulation; make progress in the Doha development trade round; bring closer EU membership for Turkey, the Balkans and Eastern Europe; and improve the focus and quality of EU aid so it better helps the poorest countries.

We will continue to lead European defence cooperation. We will build stronger EU defence capabilities, in harmony with NATO – the cornerstone of our defence policy – without compromising our national ability to act independently. We will ensure the new EU battle groups are equipped and organised to act quickly to save lives in humanitarian crises.

On the euro, we maintain our common-sense policy. The determining factor underpinning any government decision is the national economic interest and whether the case for joining is clear and unambiguous. The five economic tests must be met before any decision to join can be made. If the Government were to recommend joining, it would be put to a vote in Parliament and a referendum of the British people.

■ Protecting British interests and British citizens abroad

We will continue to provide effective support to British businesses and trade unions abroad, and we will continue to improve our ability to respond quickly to international crises and disasters which affect our citizens. The Foreign Office already provides a wide range of services for British people in difficulty overseas, and we will consult widely before drawing up a comprehensive statement spelling out the rights and responsibilities of British travellers abroad. This will include the help that people can expect from their government in times of need.

■ Helping make you more secure

We have worked closely with the US and other nations to combat the threat of terrorism in Afghanistan and in Iraq. The threat of the proliferation of chemical, biological and nuclear weapons – and their use by rogue states or terrorist groups – is a pressing issue for the world today. We have worked with the US to ensure that Libya has given up its WMD, and we will continue with France and Germany to ensure that Iran does not develop nuclear weapons. In North Korea we will support the multilateral approach of the Six Parties talks. We will continue to strongly support the peace process between India and Pakistan, and back moves to resolve the long-running dispute over Kashmir. And we will work to put an end to the international network of trade in weapons of mass destruction. Labour has already introduced a strict regime to control the export of conventional weapons, and we led moves for EU-wide measures. We will work actively to secure an international treaty on the arms trade.

■ Promoting human rights, peace and democracy

We need to be tough on terrorism and its causes. The threat of terrorism and the danger to British citizens is proven, not just by September 11th but by repeated attacks in Europe and around the world. So we cannot sit back and hope that we will be unaffected. It is right that we do everything in our power to disrupt terrorist networks, and to challenge the conditions that help terrorism to breed.

The UN Charter proclaims the universal principles of human rights and democracy. In an uncertain world they are not only right in principle, they are important guarantees of our national security and prosperity too.

'Domestic interests and international action are entwined more than ever before. Action on drugs, terrorism, people trafficking, AIDS, climate change, poverty, migration and trade all require us to work with other countries and through international organisations.'

There have been major strides forward in recent years: in Indonesia, Afghanistan and many parts of Africa and Latin America, democracy is being extended.

We mourn the loss of life of innocent civilians and coalition forces in the war in Iraq and the subsequent terrorism. But the butchery of Saddam is over and across Iraq, eight million people risked their lives to vote earlier this year. Many people disagreed with the action we took in Iraq. We respect and understand their views. But we should all now unite to support the fledgling democracy in Iraq. British troops should remain in Iraq under a United Nations mandate as long as the democratically elected government there wants them. They will continue to train Iraqi security forces to take responsibility for their own future.

We welcome the wider process of democratic reform across the Middle East, and we will work with our allies to encourage and promote economic and political change.

We strongly support the peace process between Israel and Palestine. Resolution of the conflict is crucial to peace in the region and the wider world. The conference held in London in March 2005 has started the process of helping a democratic government in Palestine build security and prosperity. We will work tirelessly to bring about a peace settlement in which a viable and independent state of Palestine lives alongside a safe and secure Israel.

■ Supporting our armed forces

Britain's armed forces are among the best in the world. They are able to play a key role in advancing our interests and values. We want to keep it that way.

We are immensely proud of the bravery, skill and dedication our armed forces have demonstrated in Afghanistan, Iraq, Sierra Leone, the

Balkans and elsewhere across the world. They are a force for good. We will never commit forces to battle unless it is essential; but when they are committed they will have the investment, strategy, training and preparation they need. That is one reason we have given the armed forces the biggest sustained increase in funding since the end of the Cold War. But we also know that modern demands on our armed forces are changing. That is why reform and modernisation are essential. A reduction in the number of infantry battalions, made possible because of the improved security situation in Northern Ireland, has allowed extra resources for the vital support services such as signals, engineers, intelligence and logistics units – the parts of the army most under pressure. This is essential to allow our infantry soldiers to be fully supported when they go into action on our behalf. We will continue with the investment and reform that make our fighting forces the most flexible and effective in the world.

We are also committed to retaining the independent nuclear deterrent and we will continue to work, both bilaterally and through the UN, to urge states not yet party to non-proliferation treaties, notably the Nuclear Non-Proliferation Treaty, to join.

■ Veterans
Labour has always recognised the sacrifice and bravery of our servicemen and women. That is why we were the first government to appoint a Minister for Veterans Affairs. This has enabled us to put veterans' affairs at the heart of decision-making at the Ministry of Defence. Labour has also put more money than ever before into veterans' issues, including £27 million of Lottery funding over the last two years. We will continue to give priority to veterans' affairs as we mark 60 years since the end of the Second World War.

■ Reforming the United Nations
The UN is crucial to our efforts to build a more secure and more

prosperous world. We support the reform of the Security Council so it becomes more representative and has a stronger focus on conflict prevention. We support the recommendation of the Secretary-General's High-level Panel for a Peace-building Commission to assist countries emerging from conflict and to develop mechanisms to enhance conflict prevention. We will press for more radical reform of the UN humanitarian system, so it is better equipped to saves lives. We will also press for reform of the World Bank and IMF to improve transparency, give more say to developing countries and, with the EU better focus their efforts on the poorest countries, particularly in Africa.

■ Climate change and Africa

Britain has the chair of the G8 this year. We will use the summit for two particular purposes.

First, climate change is the one of the most pressing challenges that the world faces. We will continue to lead internationally on climate change, and to strive for wider acceptance of the science and the steps needed to combat the problem. We will look beyond Kyoto and promote an international dialogue to reach agreement on the long-term goals and action needed to stabilise the level of greenhouse gases in the atmosphere. We will also work for effective international action to adapt to the impacts of climate change.

The UK has already met its obligations under the Kyoto Protocol. We remain committed to achieving a 20 per cent reduction in carbon dioxide emissions on 1990 levels by 2010, and our review of progress this summer will show us how to get back on track. A 60 per cent reduction by 2050 remains necessary and achievable.

We will continue to promote and develop renewable energy sources, to seek high standards of energy efficiency in the public and private sectors, and to support emissions trading in Europe and beyond.

Secondly we will focus on Africa and the global fight against poverty.

We have more than doubled aid since 1997. We have cancelled the debts of the poorest countries and are now pushing others to follow our lead and offer 100 per cent debt relief for the poorest. We are proud to have established a Department for International Development, with a clear mission to reduce poverty. Now, for the first time ever the UK has a clear timetable – 2013 – for achieving the UN target of 0.7 per cent of national income devoted to development. Globally we are pressing for a doubling of aid backed by getting international agreement to an International Finance Facility as supported by the Commission for Africa.

But aid will not be successful without conflict prevention, good governance and zero tolerance of corruption. We will work for faster repatriation of stolen assets from UK financial institutions, ratification of the UN Convention on corruption, and more open and accountable reporting of revenues from oil and mining – that so often fuel local conflicts. Our commitment is to the people of the developing world; our contract is with their governments for reform. But if poor countries are committed to good governance and poverty reduction we then believe they should be in control of their own policies. We will end the practice of making aid conditional on sensitive economic policy choices, such as trade liberalisation and privatisation.

With this leadership and extra money, we can now work to ensure all children go to school, and millions of people in Asia and Africa suffering from AIDS, tuberculosis and malaria have access to treatment. In particular, we will press for an international agreement on universal access to AIDS treatment by 2010 and for all people in poor countries to have access to free basic healthcare and education.

Our long-term aim is to help lift a billion people out of poverty.

■ Fair trade

We also know that without fairer trade rules and private investment, poor countries will not generate the growth needed to lift themselves out of poverty. We will press for the conclusion of an ambitious trade deal that will completely open markets to exports from poorer countries; for further reform of rich countries' agricultural subsidies, including the EU's Common Agricultural Policy and a 2010 timetable to end agricultural export subsidies. We do not believe poor countries should be forced to liberalise. We will allow them to sequence their trade reforms, so they can build their capacity to compete globally.

The choice for 2010

In 1997 the Tories had left Britain isolated in Europe, overseas aid had declined and we lacked any coherent vision of our place in the world. With Labour, a strong Britain will force international terrorism into retreat and help spread democracy and freedom around the world. We will be leaders in a reformed Europe, and, with others, make significant progress towards raising a billion people out of extreme poverty. We will fight for a new global agreement on climate change, an arms trade treaty, and a trade deal that makes trade work for the many, not just the few. Our armed forces will continue to be the best in the world. The alternative is to go back to the Tories with their record of cuts in aid and defence and their policies of tearing up the Social Chapter, and marginalising Britain in Europe and the world.

Chapter 8

Quality of life: Excellence for all
Forward to Olympic gold, not back
to cuts in sport and culture

1992-1997: Arts spending cut by 13 per cent
in real terms

2005: Free entry to national museums, and
visits up 75 per cent

2012: An Olympic legacy for Britain

Arts, culture and sport are thriving around Britain – enriching individual lives and transforming communities, towns and cities. They are important in their own right – as nourishment for our imagination or a source of plain enjoyment and our local environment should be a source of pride. We will work to improve the quality of life of every community in Britain.

■ The new Labour case

We believe in the inherent value of arts, culture and sport. Our towns and cities are being energised by sports and culture and as they are regenerated the quality of life for all is transformed. As we build on this change, our progressive challenge is to broaden participation as widely as possible, making the links between sport and health, and culture and well-being. We must combine the broadest base of participation with the ability for the most talented to progress to the very top. Our third term will embed the expectation that every child and every adult have the maximum chance to develop their creative or sporting talents.

■ Creative cities

Art and culture are valuable for their own sake; they are also crucial to our national prosperity. Britain's cultural industries now make up over eight per cent of our national income; and from computer games to the fine arts, British talent is gaining global recognition and generating real wealth. This is one of the fastest growing and fastest changing areas of the economy. And the transformation of our great cities is, in great part, a story of culture-led regeneration. We are proud of the record of Labour-led councils in leading this transformation, from Gateshead to Greenwich.

To help young talent get the right start we will work to establish Creative Apprenticeships. Through the National Endowment for Science, Technology and the Arts (NESTA) we are funding the Creative Pioneer Academy which will develop the entrepreneurial skills of recent graduates with outstanding talents and original business ideas – and for some there will be the offer of up to £35,000 to start their own business.

From 2006 we will provide £12 million over two years to the Arts Council England to promote leadership and management in the cultural sector. We want to invest in high-flyers developing commercial and business skills, encourage the talents of leading ethnic minority figures and improve the links between arts and business.

■ Arts, culture and museums

Since 1997 we have increased funding for the arts by 73 per cent in real terms. We will continue to support our finest artists and institutions to achieve world-class standards.

Thanks to our policy of free admissions the number of people visiting formerly charging national museums and galleries has risen by 75 per cent over three years. Many are first-time visitors, with the biggest increases among children.

Victorian City leaders left us a legacy of great local and regional museums, and through our investment programme 'Renaissance in the Regions', we are re-creating them as centres of excellence. By 2008 we will have invested £147 million in partnerships across the country, modernising museum collections, broadening access to new audiences and providing a comprehensive service to schools. We will explore further ways to encourage philanthropy to boost the quality of our public art collections.

We will legislate, as soon as time allows, to implement the findings of the Heritage Protection Review, which allows the public a greater say in listing decisions.

■ Creative Sparks

Our aim is that everyone should have the opportunity to participate in cultural life, and we want that involvement to start as early as possible. Creative Partnerships, our programme of support for art in schools in our most disadvantaged areas, has already reached over 150,000 children. We will build on this approach by rolling out our new programme Creative Sparks to guarantee that all children and young people will be given the chance to experience the very best of culture every year.

■ Sport for all

Our aim is to increase participation in sport year on year. Central to this is having modern, high-quality facilities close to where people live. £1.5 billion is being invested in sports facilities in every community. By 2008 our aim is that almost everyone will be within 20 minutes of a good multi-sport facility.

Grassroots clubs are the lifeblood of sports in Britain, and week in, week out, they are sustained by an army of volunteers. Reform of Sport England will continue, to reduce overheads and ensure that more money reaches the grassroots. We have put sports clubs at the forefront of our investment plans with the £100 million Community Club Development Scheme and mandatory rate relief at 80 per cent for registered Community Amateur Sports Clubs already worth about £5 million. As we review the operation of the new licensing regime we will ensure that there is not an unfair burden on local community groups, including sports clubs.

Investment in school sports will ensure that by 2010 all children will receive two hours high-quality PE or sport per week. Building on that, we pledge that by 2010 every child who wants it will have access to a further two to three hours sport per week.

Every child should have the chance to compete at school. We have clamped down on the sale of playing fields: 96 per cent of schools in School Sport Partnerships now hold at least one sports day or sports festival each year. All secondary schools will be expected to field teams in regular competitive fixtures. We will also establish individual and team rankings in all the main sports, with clear and transparent success criteria.

■ Sport in the community

To make it easier to get access to sports in your local area we will establish Sport Direct – a single point of access for sports in the UK. One website and one phone number will help you find out what's going on in your area. Together with £155 million from the Big Lottery Fund, the Government will ensure that children who have had little access to play facilities and those with a disability have much better access to safe, modern playgrounds.

Building on the lessons of the Football Foundation, we will develop a National Sports Foundation to bring resources from the private and voluntary sectors together with public money to invest in grassroots sporting facilities. We will work with the Premier League and the FA to find innovative ways of assisting community sport, including Supporters Direct. Having passed the necessary legislation, we remain committed to completing the sale of the Tote to a Racing Trust.

■ The Olympics

Britain's medal hauls at the Sydney Olympics in 2000 and in Athens in 2004 were the best for over 80 years, and we maintained our position as one of the leading nations in the Paralympics. Now we are supporting the bid to bring the Olympics to London in 2012. Our plans would bring regeneration to the East End of London and will leave lasting sporting, economic and cultural legacies. As we approach the Olympics we will continue to invest in elite athletes through the Talented Athlete Scholarship Scheme for young athletes. In addition

*'Our towns and cities
are being energised by
sports and culture and
as they are regenerated
the quality of life for
all is transformed.'*

we have launched 2012 Scholarships worth around £10,000 a year each for our most talented 12- to 18-year-olds.

■ Libraries in the information age

Where they offer new services like childcare, after-school education for pupils, and IT learning our libraries are successful. We will develop a strategy for the modernisation of our libraries which builds on the best, strengthens library leadership, sharpens customer focus and harnesses local popular support. We will encourage further cooperation in back-office functions and identify the best ways to improve our library infrastructure.

■ Public service broadcasting and the BBC

We support a strong, independent and world-class BBC with clearly defined public purposes at the heart of a healthy public broadcasting system. We will replace the BBC Governors with a BBC Trust to ensure that the BBC's governance and regulation is accountable to the licence-fee payers to whom it belongs. The licence fee will be guaranteed for the whole of the ten-year Royal Charter that will take effect on 1 January 2007. Channel 4 will continue to be a publicly owned broadcaster providing distinctive competition to the BBC. ITV and Five will also be retained in our public service broadcasting system.

■ Digital switchover

The success of satelite and cable television in driving take-up of digital shows how changes in technology bring real benefits – in terms of greater choice, and increasingly, in access to services. Our aim is to make those benefits available to all. We will achieve digital switchover between 2008 and 2012 ensuring universal access to high-quality, free-to-view and subscription digital TV. This will happen region by region, and we will make sure that the interests of elderly people and other vulnerable groups are protected.

■ Digital challenge

We will deliver our cross-government strategy for closing the digital divide and using ICT to further transform public services:

* *By 2006 every school supported to offer all pupils access to computers at home.*
* *A Digital Challenge for a local authority to be a national and international pathfinder in universal digital service provision.*
* *A new National Internet Safety Unit to make Britain the safest place in the world to access the internet.*

■ Copyright in a digital age

We will modernise copyright and other forms of protection of intellectual property rights so that they are appropriate for the digital age. We will use our presidency of the EU to look at how to ensure content creators can protect their innovations in a digital age. Piracy is a growing threat and we will work with industry to protect against it.

■ Film

The strength of Britain's film industry is a source of pride, and employment. We will continue to make the UK the right place to invest in film production. We will legislate to provide new tax reliefs that will ensure support is delivered directly and efficiently to those who produce films.

We will work with the UK Film Council to achieve a higher priority for funding film festivals around the country, in particular for the Edinburgh Film Festival, the oldest in Britain.

■ The Lottery

Every single part of British life has been touched by the £15 billion generated for good causes by the Lottery. Labour has made the Lottery more inclusive and more in tune with people's priorities. We have created the Big Lottery Fund and given it an explicit mandate to involve people not just in setting strategy but also in awarding grants. Our Lottery Bill will give a duty and a power to every Lottery distributor to involve the public more radically in decision-making at every level.

By the end of 2005 we will put in place a new, national consultation on the way that the National Lottery good causes proceeds are spent after the new Lottery Licence is awarded in 2009.

■ The local environment

The quality of our local environment is vital to our well-being and our natural environment is a key part of our national heritage.

The environment starts at the front door, and we have made action to improve the cleanliness of public spaces and communities a priority. The 2005 Clean Neighbourhoods and Environment Act will give local authorities and regulators the powers they have asked for to tackle litter, graffiti, abandoned cars, fly-tipping, noise pollution and other environmental concerns. We will further crack down on environmental crime, minimising litter, cleaning up graffiti and tackling fly-tipping. We will extend kerbside collection of at least two types of recyclable materials to all households in England by 2010. Polluters will have the opportunity to invest in environmental remediation or new local environmental projects rather than just pay fines. Rather than 'polluter pays' this new system would mean the 'polluter improves'.

Britain's beaches, rivers and drinking water are now of the highest ever quality. We have added 30,000 hectares to the green belt while exceeding our target of building 60 per cent of new houses on brownfield sites. We have established the first National Park in England since the 1950s. To enhance our children's understanding of the environment we will give every school student the opportunity to experience out-of-classroom learning in the natural environment.

All newly developed communities – such as the Thames Gateway Development – will be built to high environmental standards on issues such as energy efficiency and water use, and we will develop a clear plan to minimise the impact of new communities on the environment. From April 2006, all new homes receiving government funding will meet the new Code for Sustainable Buildings and we will encourage local authorities to apply similar standards to private homes.

Through a Marine Act, we will introduce a new framework for the seas, based on marine spatial planning, that balances conservation, energy and resource needs. To obtain best value from different uses of our valuable marine resources, we must maintain and protect the ecosystems on which they depend.

The choice for 2010

The Tories have always neglected the arts, seeing them as an easy target for cuts. They do not understand the role that culture can play in the lives of individuals, in the futures of our towns and cities, and in the prosperity of our country. The choice is forward with new Labour to more sport in schools, arts for all children and young people, and continued investment in culture. Or back to the Tories and cuts of £207 million across culture, arts and sport.

Chapter 9

Democracy: Power devolved,
citizens empowered
Forward to reform and
decentralisation not back to
opportunism and neglect

1979-1997:	Power centralised to Whitehall
1997-2005:	Power devolved to Scotland, Wales, London
2010:	Stronger local government, with local communities able to make the key decisions about their own neighbourhoods

In our first two terms we enshrined a new constitutional settlement between the nations of the United Kingdom. In our next term we will complete the reform of the House of Lords so that it is a modern and effective revising Chamber. And we will devolve more power to local authorities and local communities, giving people real power over the issues that matter most to them.

■ The new Labour case

Widening access to power is as important as widening access to wealth and opportunity. National standards are important to ensure fairness. But the best way to tackle exclusion is to give choice and power to those left behind. Our political institutions – including our own party – must engage a population overloaded with information, diverse in its values and lifestyles, and sceptical of power. However, people are passionate about politics – when they see it affects them. So our challenge is to bridge the chasm between government and governed. Our third term will build upon our unprecedented programme of constitutional reform embedding a culture of devolved government at the centre and self-government in our communities.

■ Building from the neighbourhood up

People want a sense of control over their own neighbourhood. Not a new tier of neighbourhood government, but new powers over the problems that confront them when they step outside their front door – issues like litter, graffiti and anti-social behaviour. That is why we will offer neighbourhoods a range of powers from which they can choose, including:

* *New powers for parish councils to deal with anti-social behaviour.*
* *Powers for local people to trigger action in response to persistent local problems.*
* *Community funds for local neighbourhoods to spend on local priorities.*

103

'Widening access to power is as important as widening access to wealth and opportunity. National standards are important to ensure fairness.'

New opportunities for communities to assume greater responsibility or even ownership of community assets like village halls, community centres, libraries or recreational facilities.

Good parish councils engage communities and make a real difference, so we will extend the right to establish parish councils to communities in London.

■ A vibrant civil society

We believe that enterprises in the mutual and cooperative sector have an important role to play in the provision of local services, from health to education, from leisure to care for the vulnerable. As democratic, not-for-profit organisations, they can help to involve local people in shaping the services they want, unleash creativity and innovation, create jobs and provide new services – especially in neighbourhoods where traditional services have failed local people in the past.

We have introduced a new legal form – the Community Interest Company (CIC) – and want to support new enterprises. As a major stimulus to this sector, central government and local authorities will work with these 'social enterprises' wherever possible. Where services can be provided by mutuals, cooperatives or CICs to the required standards of quality and value for money, they should be positively encouraged to develop and be included in procurement policies. We will discuss with local authorities the best way to achieve this.

In a range of services the voluntary and community sector has shown itself to be innovative, efficient and effective. Its potential for service delivery should be considered on equal terms. We will continue to improve the context in which the gifting of time and resources to the voluntary sector takes place. We will reintroduce the widely supported reforms in the Charities Bill.

We understand that often the spark for local innovation and change comes from one or two dedicated, visionary individuals. These people, sometimes dubbed 'social entrepreneurs', deserve our full support. We will develop a framework of incentives and rewards, to recognise the special people in every community whose voluntary efforts transform the lives of others.

■ A better alternative for young people

We know that parents and young people think that there should be more things to do and places to go for teenagers. We will publish plans to reform provision in order to ensure that all young people have access to a wider set of activities after the school day such as sport and the arts. We are determined that better provision will be allied to a stronger voice for the young themselves in designing and managing local provision. We will establish the first ever national framework for youth volunteering, action and engagement – a modern national youth community service, led by young people themselves – with an investment over the next three years of up to £100 million with matched funding from business, the voluntary sector and the Lottery.

■ Councils: more freedom, less bureaucracy

Strong communities ultimately require strong local government. We will give councils further freedoms to deliver better local services, subject to minimum national standards, with even greater freedoms for top-performing councils. We will reduce unnecessary bureaucracy by cutting both the cost of inspection and the total number of inspectorates, and we will dramatically simplify the many funding streams available to local areas through new Local Area Agreements. We will also give councils greater stability by providing three-year funding. We will continue to deliver efficiency savings and improvements to local services through joint procurement, shared services, streamlining administrative structures while promoting decision-making at the level that will make a difference. We will continue to strengthen the

community leadership role of local authorities working in partnership
with public, voluntary and private bodies.

■ Stronger leadership

Strong local government requires strong leadership. We will ensure
that councils are organised in the most effective way to lead and support local partnerships and deliver high-quality services. We will
explore giving people a more direct opportunity to express a view
about whether they would like to have a directly elected mayor. We will
also consult with city councils on the powers needed for a new generation of city mayors. And we will examine the case for simplifying the
current local government election cycle by moving towards 'whole
council' elections every four years.

■ Council tax under control

Labour recognises the concerns that have been raised about the level
of council tax. This year we have delivered the lowest council tax
increase in over a decade through a combination of extra investment
and tough action to cap excessive increases.

We will continue to invest in local services with year-on-year increases
in grants to local councils, and will not hesitate to use our capping
powers to protect council taxpayers from excessive rises in council tax.

We remain concerned that many council taxpayers are not claiming
reductions in their council tax bills to which they are already entitled.
We will therefore introduce measures to make it easier for pensioners
and people on low incomes to claim Council Tax Benefit.

In the longer term, we are committed to reforming council tax and will
consider carefully the conclusions of the Lyons Review into local government finance.

■ The nations and regions of the UK

In our first term, we devolved power to Scotland and Wales and restored city-wide government to London. Britain is stronger as a result. In the next Parliament, we will decentralise power further. In Wales we will develop democratic devolution by creating a stronger Assembly with enhanced legislative powers and a reformed structure and electoral system to make the exercise of Assembly responsibilities clearer and more accountable to the public. We will also review the powers of the London Mayor and the Greater London Authority. And we will devolve further responsibility to existing regional bodies in relation to planning, housing, economic development and transport.

■ Northern Ireland

The Belfast Agreement on Good Friday 1998, was a remarkable achievement. Life in Northern Ireland is immeasurably better as a result. A huge programme of reform in policing, justice and rights, together with the lowest ever unemployment has helped address the inequalities of the past and has created a new confidence.

It is unacceptable that seven years after the agreement there are still paramilitary groups involved in criminality and punishment attacks. This has to end. The period of transition is over. Unionist politicians have made it clear that they are prepared to share power with national-ists and republicans if violence is ended once and for all. It is time for all groups in Northern Ireland to make it clear they will only use dem-ocratic and peaceful means to advance their aims.

We will work tirelessly with the parties in Northern Ireland and with the Irish government to re-establish the devolved institutions. But this can only happen on an inclusive basis if the IRA ends paramilitarism and criminality for good and decommissions its weapons. Bringing this about so that normal politics can take over in the Province will be our principal aim.

'The best way to tackle exclusion is to give choice and power to those left behind.'

Loyalist paramilitary violence and criminality is equally intolerable. We will ensure that it is dealt with severely while providing the assistance necessary to Loyalist communities to ensure that prosperity is spread throughout Northern Ireland.

■ Parliamentary reform

Labour has already taken steps to make the House of Commons more representative, through all-women shortlists. Labour will also continue to support reforms that improve parliamentary accountability and scrutiny led by the successful Modernisation Committee.

In our first term, we ended the absurdity of a House of Lords dominated by hereditary peers. Labour believes that a reformed Upper Chamber must be effective, legitimate and more representative without challenging the primacy of the House of Commons.

Following a review conducted by a committee of both Houses, we will seek agreement on codifying the key conventions of the Lords, and developing alternative forms of scrutiny that complement rather than replicate those of the Commons; the review should also explore how the upper chamber might offer a better route for public engagement in scrutiny and policy-making. We will legislate to place reasonable limits on the time bills spend in the second chamber – no longer than 60 sitting days for most bills.

As part of the process of modernisation, we will remove the remaining hereditary peers and allow a free vote on the composition of the House.

Labour remains committed to reviewing the experience of the new electoral systems – introduced for the devolved administrations, the European Parliament and the London Assembly. A referendum remains the right way to agree any change for Westminster.

Having been the first government to take action to clean up the funding of political parties, we will continue to work with the independent Electoral Commission to explore how best to support the vital democratic role of political parties while recognising that campaigning activity must always be funded by parties from their own resources.

Since 1997 there has been a flowering of innovative forms of public engagement, for example, the Citizens Council used by the National Institute for Clinical Excellence to advise on ethical dilemmas. With the growing importance of new public policy issues and dilemmas – particularly those arising from scientific advances – we will continue to explore new and innovative forms of public engagement raising their profile and status in policy-making.

■ A voice for all

A fully democratic society depends on giving everyone a voice and stake. Only Labour governments have ever introduced race relations legislation, and laws passed in 2000 are ensuring that all public bodies promote diversity and tackle discrimination against black and Asian Britons. We will continue to promote civil rights for disabled people, ensuring full implementation of the new positive duty on the public sector to promote equality of opportunity for disabled people. We will also introduce a similar duty to promote equality of opportunity between women and men, and will further extend protection against discrimination on the grounds of religion and belief. We are committed to improving the rights and opportunities of gays and lesbians, that's why we brought in legislation on civil partnerships, reducing the age of consent, repealed Section 28 and reformed the sexual offences legislation so that it was no longer discriminatory.

It remains our firm and clear intention to give people of all faiths the same protection against incitement to hatred on the basis of their religion. We will legislate to outlaw it and will continue the dialogue we have started with faith groups from all backgrounds about how best to balance protection, tolerance and free speech.

We are proud to have brought in the Human Rights Act, enabling British citizens to take action in British courts rather than having to wait years to seek redress in Strasbourg. But rights must be balanced by responsibilities. So we will continue to bear down on abusive or frivolous claims.

In the next Parliament we will establish a Commission on Equality and Human Rights to promote equality for all and, tackle discrimination, and introduce a Single Equality Act to modernise and simplify equality legislation.

The choice for 2010

The Tories have only one policy on democratic reform – opportunism. Arch centralisers when in office, they now claim to be localists. Having refused for decades to accept any reform of the archaic House of Lords, some of them now claim to support a fully elected House. The choice is forward with new Labour to modern institutions and more power than ever devolved to communities and successful local authorities. Or back with the Tories to a government indifferent to the health of our democracy and negligent of our institutions.